STILL

GOING —

BLISSFULLY

LOST

IN

THE

BAJA

Barbara Thacker

copyright © 1999, Barbara Henning-Thacker
All rights reserved, including the right to
reproduce this book or any part thereof,
in any form, except for inclusion of brief
quotations in a review.

Printed in The United States of America
   First Printing, 1999
   ISBN: 0-938513-25-7
   Library of Congress Catalog # 99-72223

AMADOR PUBLISHERS
P. O. Box 12335
Albuquerque, NM 87195

[Special Imprint — **Inkwell Press**]

"The great thing about this story is that it all comes out right in the end. There is real drama, but it is of a natural sort, the drama of a thunderstorm in the desert or the last fiery stretches of sun across the vast Pacific; this drama thrills and entices, but doesn't frighten. The thing I love best about this tale is the message of fearlessness that comes with the joy of following a dream. This story illustrates beautifully how our world is largely what we create it to be. When Barb comes to call in her 'guest house' she is a real-life Parnassus on Wheels, and her tales are in the timeless tradition of adventure on the high road, appealing to the seed of imagination that lies dormant in us all."

— Dr. E.J. Struthers, Ph.D. Anthropology

"I am not an armchair traveler, I prefer to go myself. But with Barbara's book, you don't have to be anything or go anywhere. Reading this book was as easy and enthralling as her first one. I could not put it down. I can explain it by saying: Barb sits with you enjoying a cup of cota tea and takes you there in a spiritual walkabout. She's a storyteller. Under her spell people and places come to life. The barrio was as real as my own neighborhood. I want to know more about these people, their lives, and their barrio. What happened to the children? To Jorge and Elisa? To Hermalinda and Mirta? Has Todos Santos been ravished by tourism and fast food chains? Have people ceased to care about their neighbors? Do they have to lock their doors at night? Are palapas now prefab? Barb has to go back and tell us more."

— Dayl Pourraid, native of Argentina

"I first met Barbara Thacker in March of 1994, shortly after she and her dogs — Ink and Negro — had ventured alone for the second time down the Baja peninsula in a small Toyota camper which appeared less than travel-worthy.

"My first impression of Barbara was that of a woman, at age 63, comprised of equal parts fearlessness and craziness. Such a description could be applied to most any other explorer in our history. I admire Barbara for her courage to venture out, on her own, to the ends of the continent.

"Barbara's stories, detailed and precious, allow us less-adventurous types to experience the world without having to leave the comfort of our sofa. Godspeed, Barbara." — Jay P. Tharinger

THE OBSERVER NEWSPAPER, Rio Rancho, NM

"I thought I was in the passanger seat. Reading Barb's book allowed me to take a trip without leaving home. If I were asked to describe this book in three words, they would be: Descriptive, Inspirational, Touching. Barb, check the fluids and tires on Tessie. I'm ready for another trip or another book." — Carl Silva, owner

THE BOOKMARK at Placitas, NM

"Aquí tenemos una nueva autora, una mujer aventurera que sabe mirar a la belleza del ambiente alrededor. Se lo ve con los ojos del corazón."

— Christina Tomlinson, maestra de español

Dedication

For all those who have read HOW CAN I BE LOST WHEN I DON'T KNOW WHERE I'M GOING?, who have written wonderful letters, who have inquired if Ink and I continued the odyssey — this one's for you. Hope you will enjoy the Baja interlude as much as we!

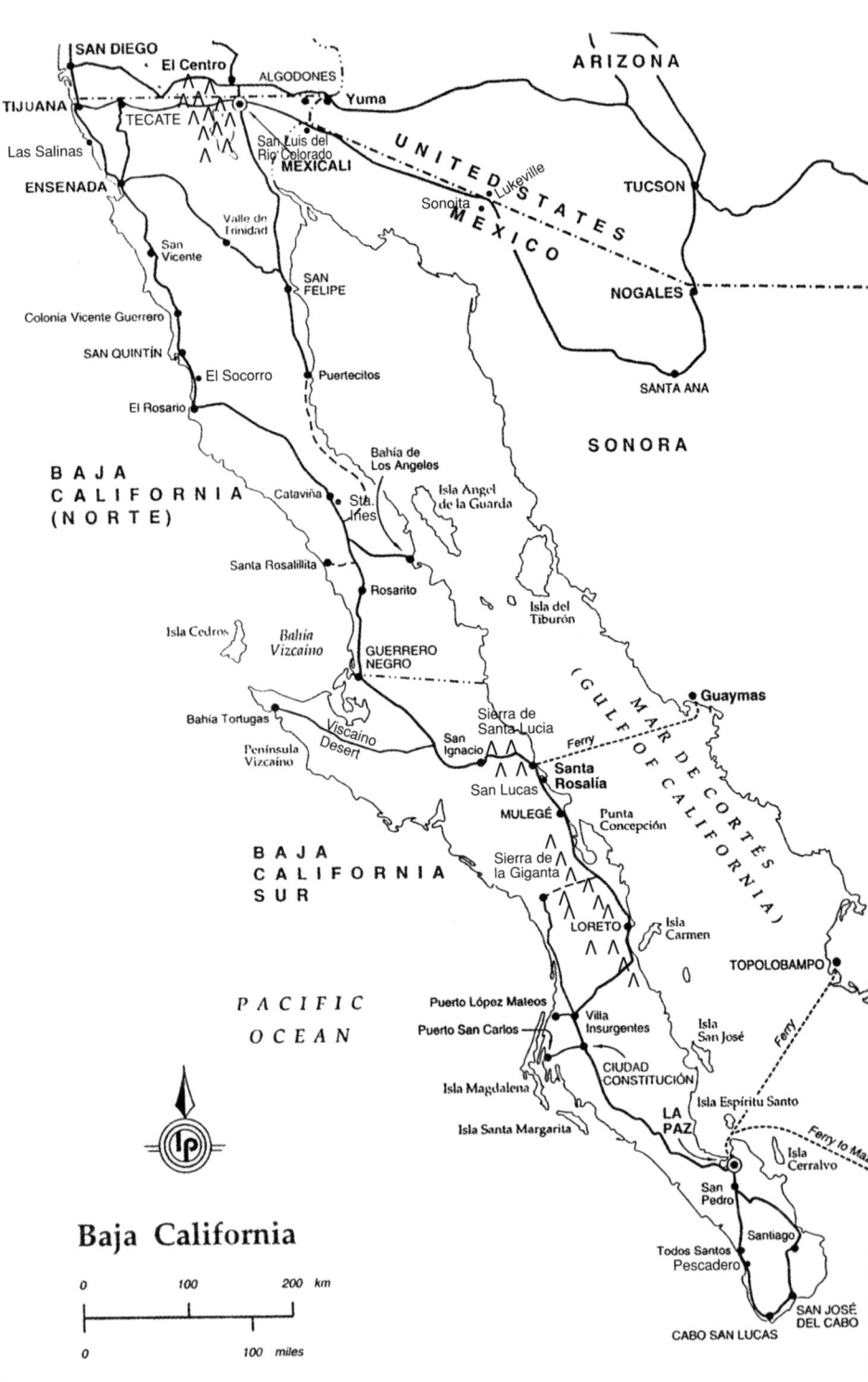

Table of Contents

Foreword	9
Westward Ho!	11
Tackling the Transpeninsular	30
The Beach	51
Life in Barrio San Ignacio	86
North on the Transpeninsular	188
Back Home Once More	199

Foreword

For those who have not read *How Can I Be Lost When I Don't Know Where I'm Going?* — You should! Nevertheless, I shall list names that carry over into this second book for your clarification:

TESSIE - a 1978 Toyota Chinook. "Tessie Toyota" carried us safely and well on a journey of 26 months and 31,00 miles.

SAMANTHA - a Graduate student at New Mexico State University, Sam and her daughter Thelonika were my extended family in Las Cruces.

INK - My faithful travel companion. Half English Springer and half Gorden Setter, Ink is a big, black dog with not one mean bone in her body.

PAM - Pam Smith works for the BLM in Las Cruces, NM, and is another extended family member. Pam kept the mail flowing for the entire 26 months I was on the road.

MARK - my younger son, living in Oak Ridge, TN, who understood completely my need to make this odyssey since he, too, has an adventurous nature. He and his wife, Lois, were constant supporters of my wild adventure.

MARY - a wise, wonderful woman. Mary made baby clothes for me before I was born. A surrogate mother since my own mother died when I was ten, Mary has nutured me all my life.

SCOT - my older son, living in Irvine, CA with his wife Juli. Scot could not relate to his mother becoming a gypsy, but always sent words of encouragement.

Westward Ho!

On January 6, 1989, the gypsy caravan left Las Cruces once again — this time heading west.

It had been a different Holiday season. I had never spent Christmas in a camper before. The only decoration was a small cloth tree hanging on Tessie's door. Since we were parked behind Samantha's house, we had a steady stream of visitors. Ink had new puppies to entertain her. The season was sufficiently festive.

Tessie did not lend herself to entertaining more than three people, so I invited a group to luncheon at Mesilla Valley Inn. It was there that I announced that I was not ready to give up life on the open road and would be heading out once again. I'm sure there were some who questioned why anyone would want to roam around in a camper. I knew, however, I must continue this wonderful adventure. To the query, where are you going now? I could only answer — West. As good friends do, they accepted my decision and wished me well. It was a nice gathering and an opportunity to see and visit with many friends.

I purchased two Christmas presents for the caravan: a portable Brother electric typewriter and a small quartz heater that was adequate to take the chill off. Two necessary gifts that would ease life greatly. Tessie's present was a full day in the garage and a complete check-up. Ink settled for turkey and stuffing at Christmas dinner.

With the New Year, we pulled stakes at Sam's. She had

been so kind to have us and coined a phrase I loved. When I said, "Sam, it's time for you to be rid of this house guest." Sam countered with, "Oh, Barb, you're not a house guest, you're a guest house."

Then it was a few days parked in Pam's driveway. We did some serious soaking in the jacuzzi. Of course, Pam said she'd continue to forward mail. We both agreed we liked this arrangement, since I'd phone occasionally to let Pam know where I was. What a blessing good friends are!

Spent those last few days with Pam getting Tessie rearranged, shopping for supplies, and preparing for the journey west. I even managed to finish a sweater I had been working on for Mark for two years. Strange, I had knit constantly when I was married. Now I never seemed to have the time nor the inclination. Of course, I never sat in front of a television set any longer.

Pam and I hugged a fond farewell that Friday morning. A bit of *deja-vu*; however, this time I didn't feel the stress of that first breaking away. I knew the joys of the open road now and was looking forward to seeking more bliss.

We stopped at the Fairacres Post Office and mailed out Mark's overdue sweater, then pulled onto the highway. The odometer read 51,230 miles. Headed west on I-25 for Pancho Villa State Park in Columbus, New Mexico.

It was an hour's run to Deming where we headed south on NM 11 for the 35 mile drive to Pancho Villa. Arrived about 4 p.m. and chose a site with electricity in the far south corner of the park. There weren't many campers, but the birds were abundant and the cacti beautiful. I had chosen Pancho Villa because I had a heavy cold and I needed a few days of R and R before doing any serious driving. I knew this was a peaceful place.

It was quiet and serene. Ink and I walked and watched the birds. She had trouble with all the stickers, but solved

Westward Ho!

that problem by hopping onto the picnic table at our site and stretching out there. Each night the hooty owls sang a mournful song as we looked south to the lights of Palomas, Mexico.

This New Mexico State park was originally Camp Furlong which was raided by Pancho Villa and his troops on March 9, 1916. Eight soldiers and two civilians were killed in the raid. It served as a supply depot for "Blackjack" Pershing's punitive expedition into Mexico in pursuit of Villa. After 11 months, he gave up on catching the elusive Pancho Villa and his *Villistas*. There are still remnants of Camp Furlong scattered across the fields. There's an interesting museum in the old railroad station across the road from the campground.

I played with the typewriter, who had become "Little Brother". Learned quickly why it had been so reasonably priced. The cassette ribbons were a one-shot item. No re-using them. I tried to rewind the ribbon, but no go. We drove into Deming on Wednesday and checked for ribbons to no avail. Tried to call Pam from three different phones and none worked. When we got back to Columbus, I found an operable telephone and put in a cry for help. I knew Walmart had the ribbons. Pam calmed me with, "I'll pick up some ribbons and drive over on Thursday."

The temperature that Wednesday night dropped to 11 degrees. I pulled Tessie's canvas top down and let the quartz heater hum all night. Ink and I were very snug curled up together. So, I was delighted with the heater, but not sure about "Little Brother."

# # #

Pam arrived about 3:30 p.m. on Thursday with ribbons and her dogs, Kahlua and Sweet Pea. The weather was frigid and quite windy. The water faucet at my site never thawed all day. However, we took the dogs for a brisk walk. Then, we hopped into Tessie for dinner, another visit, and another last good-bye. As we hugged, I assured Pam I would stay in touch and thanked her for being such a wonderful friend.

# # #

We moved on west on the 15th en route to Naco, Arizona, to visit John Mitchell. I felt I needed to show him that this little Toyota was as good as he had told me when I bought her from him. I had called John and he insisted that we stop and stay with him for a few days.

The drive from Columbus on Route 9 across the boot heel of New Mexico is wild, beautiful country. There are even a few miles of unpaved road. We wandered through Hachita and Animas then took Route 80 south through Rodeo and on into Arizona.

We had to stop at an inspection station north of Douglas. Arizona has a ban on fruits, vegetables, and plants coming into the state. I assured the inspector that I had nothing in the way of forbidden fruits and vegetables. Then he spied my green plant sitting in the sink and told me, "Oh, you can't bring that live plant into Arizona." By this time, I had gotten out of Tessie. In my most beguiling manner, I said, "But, Sir, that little plant has been with us for 12,000 miles. I just can't part with it."

He looked a little hesitant and asked, "Where did you get that plant?"

"It was a gift from a dear friend in Las Cruces. It's been with us for all of our travels in the eastern United States. It really loves to travel and we treasure it." By this time, I had a small tear welling up.

The dear man patted my shoulder, then dashed into the office to return with a bag of potting soil. We pulled Little Plant out of its pot, shook the roots free, and re-planted it in new soil. The inspector said, "She's okay now. Take your plant with you and good travels." We waved as we pulled away from the inspection station still carrying our spot of green.

Got to John's about 4 p.m. and found him as delightful as ever. His health was failing, but not his sense of humor. He still had a herd of dogs — seven — of all sizes and descriptions. Ink did her vamp trick, romped and played with all of them. She even pigged out on the pile of bones in the backyard. That was a mistake. Ink was sick as a dog from all that munching and spent the night urpping.

# # #

We stayed with John and his herd until the 18th, but knew we needed a warmer, quieter place so decided to drive on south and check out Patagonia Lake State Park.

Patagonia was directly west of Sierra Vista, but there was no direct route. We drove north to Huachuca City, where we took Route 82 curving through lush cattle country. There were large trees and lots of green fields which meant lots of water in this area. Found the small town of Patagonia charming, but did not tarry. Came to a sign for the State Park and drove four miles on a gravel road to the entrance. When we saw that jewel of a lake, we knew we had found another perfect spot.

There weren't many campers this time of year. I signed up for a site with electricity. I knew we'd need the heater. I could also use the toaster oven and the electric typewriter. Hadn't broken away from all the creature comforts I'd grown accustomed to in Las Cruces.

That first night at the Lake, Ink fussed and woke me. The moon was almost full and I looked out to see what was troubling my gal. There in the silvery light, right next to Tessie, was the biggest badger I had ever seen. Down in a small cove were five deer grazing. Ink growled softly, but didn't disturb the critters. We sat and watched them for quite a while.

Each evening about sunset, a doe strolled down the lane above us with twin fawns. Ink would sit and watch them intently. She seemed to understand that she shouldn't frighten them. Or, perhaps, she remembered Lucky Buck at the KOA near Corpus Cristi. We both enjoyed this closeness with the wild creatures.

There were nice trails to hike, a small marina with a working telephone, and the few campers were friendly. Jean and Newt Roepke were parked next to us. Newt was a fisherman. One evening he brought me three pan-sized trout. I fried them for dinner. Trout is my favorite fish and I really appreciated Newt's generosity as I ate that gourmet meal.

We stayed until the 25th. It was warm and pleasant and there was lots to watch and savor. I did make use of the phone. Called the Harnetts and Jeff Wilson, all in Tucson. Assured them we would touch base when we came through their fair city.

# # #

Drove south toward Nogales where we picked up Route 19 for an easy run north to Tucson. Stopped and wandered through Tumacacori National Monument. This mission was a northern outpost of a mission chain established by the Jesuits in what was then the province of Sonora. Father Kino, a German-educated Italian Jesuit, explored much of this region. He proved that lower California was a peninsula. He explored and mapped the Upper Pima country until his death in 1711. It was Father Gutierrez, a Spanish Franciscan, who arrived at Tumacacori in 1794, who determined to rebuild the church which was in ruins. He stayed until his death in 1820. Although his church was never finished, it stands today as a monument to his vision and endeavors.

After that break, we breezed through Green Valley and on into Tucson. I got some supplies and some money. We parked up at a wide open campground on the east side called Cactus Country. Not many people here either, but miles of mesa country for Ink and me to walk. I stored all the groceries, then we set out for a nice hike. The weather was changing — winds rising and clouds scudding over the Catalina Mountains.

I settled Ink after dinner and hiked up to the telephones. Called Jeff who was doing Graduate work at University of Arizona. Jeff and Mark had roomed together at NM Tech after coming over from California. He was like another son. Also, touched base with the Harnetts who had worked with us in real estate in Tucson and had remained good and loyal friends throughout the years.

Jeff and I had a super visit over dinner in Tessie Thursday evening. He never left until 10:30 but gave me some helpful input on Alaska. Jeff had worked for the Geologic Survey in Alaska the previous summer. I longed to see that state but worried about tackling those vast stretches all alone. Had visions of some grizzly eating me and Ink for dinner. Jeff advised me not to drive it. He said there would be nothing left of Tessie by the time I reached the lower states. He suggested instead taking a boat to Alaska. Hope someday to get there. After talking with Jeff, knew it would not be in my camper.

The 27th dawned rainy and cloudy. There was snow on the mountains and the wind was cold. Got the caravan together and drove over to visit with Helen and Jim Harnett.

Helen and I went to Little Molina's for a great Mexican meal. Jim was tied up with business, but managed to join us for some delicious food. Drove back to the condo and sat and visited all afternoon. Helen could not relate to my tooling around the country in a little camper. She was interested even though she stated she'd never consider doing such a thing. I assured her it wasn't every woman's cup of tea, but it was right for me. It was a raw day. The kind meant for sitting and visiting with a good friend.

Ink and I were back at the campground in time for a long walk. Even though it was cold, I knew I had to give Ink some extra attention since she had had to stay in Tessie while I played. Had a light dinner and turned in early to the hum of the heater and the howling of the wind.

# # #

We got away from Cactus Country about 11 a.m. I was to meet my Mary at her friend LaVerne's in Tempe on Sunday. LaVerne had been a neighbor in Pennsylvania before she and her husband moved to Arizona. Now they were both widows. To escape the dark, dismal, damp, depressing days of January through March in the east, Mary moves in with LaVerne. It's a great arrangement for both of them. Of course, I had to touch base with my Mary.

The trip north was uneventful. Once out of Tucson's sprawl, Route 89 was peaceful and scenic. It's called the Pinal Parkway. After Oracle Junction, there's no traffic, no towns, just open road through desert scenery. We were humming along when we spotted a big monument at the edge of a roadside park. This had to be a good place for lunch and stretching our legs. We pulled in. Discovered the monument was Tom Mix sitting astride his horse Tony. Whoa! When I was a kid, he was my Saturday afternoon movie idol. What nice luncheon companions. One of America's favorite cowboys and his horse.

We wandered on up Route 89 to Florence. I had to visit Casas Grandes. That was the afternoon expedition. I walked the grounds looking at the old adobe buildings.

Found it jarring that the Casa Grande was now covered by a big metal shelter. Wondered what the ancients would think of that. I was told it was to protect those fragile four stories from plane vibrations.

The Casa Grande is the most prominent — and the most perplexing — structure of this prehistoric Hohokam village. No one knows whether it was a ceremonial building, an ancient astronomical observatory or something else. It was constructed about 650 years ago here in the Gila Valley and is still a mystery today.

The culture of the Hohokam is distinguished by several characteristics: they lived in small scattered villages of separated single-room houses built of mud and brush; cremated their dead; were adept at carving shell and stone; and had distinctive buff-colored pottery with red designs. Their greatest achievement was an irrigation system in the Salt and Gila Valleys with more than 600 miles of canals ranging from two to six feet wide and about three feet deep. Their crops included cotton, corn, beans, and squash.

That they were influenced by the cultures of Mexico is apparent in the presence of ball courts, platform mounds on which small structures were built, pottery vessel forms and designs, copper bells, and items of decoration. Ball courts found as far north as Wupatki National Monument near Flagstaff show that the ball games and ceremonies were adopted by other southwestern people. It's not known how the game was played.

The Casa Grande, built about 1350, was abandoned by 1450 for reasons not fully understood. Perhaps a change in the weather pattern affected irrigation and the tribe moved to seek farmland closer to the river. Pressure from enemies does not seem to be a factor, since there is little evidence of warfare. Cultural similarities indicate that the Pima Indians, living nearby, may be descendants of the

Hohokam.

When I returned to the parking lot, I let Ink out for a run. She immediately went over to the grassy depression which had been the ball court. She nosed around, took care of business, but did not play any ball.

We hung it up that evening in a "sardine effect" park in Coolidge. Did laundry and had a hot shower.

# # #

Left the cramped campground early. When we got to Apache Junction, decided to take a scenic drive. We headed up the Apache Trail into the Tonto National Forest. Drove around a group of lovely little lakes. Didn't go as far as Theodore Roosevelt Dam, but it was clear that Arizona has more water than New Mexico. We parked and strolled around Canyon Lake. There were lots of people. It was a Sunday afternoon and the weather was balmy. I had a bite to eat sitting there enjoying all that water. Then we caught Route 82 straight into Tempe.

Arrived at LaVerne's about 3:30 p.m. The directions were good and I managed to find the place with only a few unnecessary circles until I got my bearings.

The streets in the neighborhood were quite narrow. LaVerne, said, "You can't hurt the grass and we don't want you out on the street, so just pull into the front yard." Which I did. It was a level parking space and out of traffic. So we settled down in LaVerne's front yard for a small stay with my Mary and her friend.

Ink was a little out of joint with LaVerne declaring the house off-limits. The back yard was fenced and she lounged there, but kept a close eye on all of us through the patio doors. She didn't understand why she couldn't be inside. However, the evening walk to the local park with Mary and me plus an extra hug when we settled in for the night, kept her in good spirits.

Westward Ho!

Mary, LaVerne, and I settled into a slow routine of visiting, doing laundry, eating, hugging, and all those womanly things. LaVerne's health was failing and Mary drove her to doctor appointments. She had use of the car, so we were able to dash around Tempe and Phoenix.

I had washed Tessie's curtains in a bucket at Patagonia one warm, sunny day. Got them cleaner, but noticed they were rotting away. The sun and long years of use were doing a number — they were threadbare. One evening we were sitting on the back patio and I asked Mary, "Do you suppose we could make new curtains for Tessie while I'm here? You're the expert on sewing, not me." LaVerne mentioned that she didn't have a sewing machine, but knew her next door neighbor owned one. We checked with the neighbor, and she graciously lent her machine. Mary giggled, "Sure, we can do this!" Next day we bought material and Mary started new curtains for Tessie.

I touched base with Mark and Lois. Scot even checked in. I had been leaving messages and moving on. He finally reached me at LaVerne's. We agreed that I would be seeing him before too long. I was slowly meandering towards California. And, of course, the mail came through thanks to Pam.

Mary and I spent one afternoon at Heard Museum. With my interest in anthropology, Heard was like a candy shop. It's not a big museum, but it has a permanent Southwest collection that contains more than 35,000 objects ranging from ancient to contemporary pots, textiles, baskets, jewelry, and kachinas. This internationally recognized collection is housed in a charming Spanish Colonial Revival building with white adobe walls and red tile roofs. There's a shady sculpture garden, the kachina gallery, pottery galore — all well labeled and displayed in spacious rooms. Mary and I browsed, sat in the garden, visited the gift shop, and enjoyed the afternoon.

While Mary worked on the curtains, I worked on Tessie's top right there in the front yard. Scrubbed the inside and outside then put a coat of Armorall on both sides. People would stop and visit. No one seemed to mind a camper parked in a yard in the neighborhood. The weather was delightful. Ink had resigned herself to loafing in the back yard. It was a quality time.

Got the camper spic and span. Then invited Mary and LaVerne out for lunch one day. We had to shove LaVerne a bit to get her up that big step, but we all settled in and ate. LaVerne had never been in a camper before and was quite impressed with my Tessie.

On Saturday, February 4, we hung the new curtains. I had picked up edging with a colorful southwestern design. It really set off the light, opaque material that Mary had chosen. Tessie looked brand new. Those curtains did a lot for her. Mary had done her usual professional job. We all were pleased.

Much as I loved being with those two wonderful, supportive women, I knew it was time to roll on down the road. I had decided I should see Organ Pipe Cactus National Monument. On Sunday, I pulled down Tessie's top, secured everything and moved out of LaVerne's front yard. It was noon before we left.

# # #

We took Interstate 10 south, cut cross-country to Casa Grande, the town, not the monument. Connected with Interstate 8 and stayed on it until Gila Bend. It was cloudy and rainy, a good day for driving. Had good jazz playing and the windshield wipers clicking. The gypsy caravan was on the road again.

At Gila Bend, it was Route 85 straight south through uninhabited country marked on my map as restricted air

Westward Ho! 23

force range. We drove through the charming village of Ajo in the rain. Decided to spend the night in Why, since that's always a good question. In spite of the rain, Ink and I did a tour of the park. Settled in for the night early. We needed the quartz heater and did not even question why here in Why, Arizona.

It was a short hop down to Organ Pipe. The sun was beaming and all seemed fine in our world. Pulled into Monument headquarters. Availed myself of all the information I thought we would need in this fabulous Sonoran desert setting. Learned a lot at headquarters including how Why got its name. It's located 22 miles north of the visitor's center. The town was originally called Rocky Point Junction. Later, it was referred to as the "Y' because of the fork in the road created by the junctions of Highways 85 and 86. When the post office was established in 1970, the name was changed to "Why" to accommodate the postal officials.

Whereas Big Bend National Park is Chihuahuan desert, Organ Pipe is Sonoran desert — a much more lush environment — and in my opinion the most beautiful of the deserts in the United States. I was looking forward to checking it out. Spent time reading about the various flora and fauna of this region.

Foremost among the desert dwellers who have mastered this harsh environment are the cacti. There are 26 species in Organ Pipe including the saguaro, and of course, the monument's namesake, the organ pipe cactus. This large cactus is found rarely in the U.S. although it's common in Mexico. The monument encompasses the bulk of the US population. It's a glutton for heat and light; therefore, it grows on south-facing slopes where it can absorb the most sun. This position is critical during the winter months when severe frosts can kill it. It blooms in the heat of May, June, and July, but the organ pipe waits until the sun goes down to open its tender lavender-white flowers.

The monument is a study in extremes of temperatures. The average maximum for January is 67 degrees, but the lowest temperature recorded is 14. In July, the average maximum is 103 with the highest temperature recorded 116. There are two distinct rainy seasons — one in mid-winter, the other in mid-summer. It is these two rainy seasons that make the Sonoran Desert so lush when compared to most other deserts, even though average yearly rainfall in only 8.73 inches. Organ Pipe is approximately 516 square miles and was established in April, 1937 by proclamation of Franklin Delano Roosevelt.

In reading further, I learned that cacti are much more widely distributed than most people think. There are cacti in all the contiguous states except Maine, New Hampshire, and Vermont.

The organ pipe cacti branch from the ground, but the saguaro have a single trunk. There's no way to tell exactly how old a cactus is unless you know when it started growing. Unlike trees, cacti don't have annual growth rings. With the saguaro, it is 70 to 80 years old before it puts out arms.

This remote region allows the life of the Sonoran Desert to flourish under nearly ideal wilderness conditions. It's an outstanding natural preserve where one of the Earth's major ecosystems survives almost unspoiled. The United States in 1976 designated the Monument as an International Biosphere Reserve.

I read about the scenic drives and, again, thanked my lucky stars for such a sweet, little camper. The two scenic loop roads were described as winding, up-and-down graded dirt roads. Motorhomes over 25 feet were prohibited and trailers were not recommended. None of this applied to

Tessie, so we headed up the 21 mile Ajo Mountain Drive. Viewed impressive stands of organ pipe cactus and the jagged peaks of the Ajo Range which is the highest in the area. Stopped at the top of the loop. From the picnic area, had a great view of a natural arch in the mountain side. Ink and I wandered around in this serene setting. We enjoyed the special silence that goes with desert solitaire. Saw only five cars on the entire journey. It was a rough road and slow going. Reminded us of Old Maverick Road in Big Bend. Tessie rumbled and rattled, but we had no problems.

Spent the night at Gringo Gulch in Lukeville. Loved the name and needed electricity which the monument campground did not have. This park was right next to a chain link fence which divided the United States from Mexico. Ink and I walked through an arroyo and lush vegetation to open space for a hike and a welcome stretch. We both wondered if anyone would have known they were strolling on the border of two different nations had it not been for that fence. Certainly, the birds did not seem to notice as they flew easily from one country to another

It was a cool, windy night at Gringo Gulch. Next morning, I decided we should do part of the Puerto Blanco Drive. I wanted to see Quitobaquito Springs. I sipped coffee and watched the birds for a while. The reassuring hum of the heater was music to my ears. We were as far south as we could be in the United States and the weather was still cold.

Got squared away and drove out a rough, untrafficked road to the Springs. This road paralleled another chain link fence which made me very aware that Mexico was just to our left. There were a few vehicles in the parking lot, so I left Ink to guard the house. I hiked an easy trail — lush and green — to the spring. Was glad Ink was not with me for she would have been swimming in that lovely, clear pond created by Quitobaquito Spring. It was a beautiful and unexpected oasis in the middle of the desert.

Got back to Lukeville early. This small settlement on the border consisted of a general store, a gasoline station, a post office, a laundromat, and a Border Patrol Station. In looking at the map, I questioned driving back north on Route 85 to Gila Bend when Route 2 in Mexico skirted the border and would bring us to Yuma by way of San Luis, Mexico. It looked good to me and Ink was always agreeable. I stopped at the General Store and bought a 24-hour Mexican Insurance policy for the next day.

The insurance policy was enlightening. The big expense and, obviously, the big concern of the Mexican insurers is the third party — namely, that you have insurance to cover damages and medical expenses in case of an accident. It is a necessary document when driving Mexican highways, since Mexico does not recognize any US insurers. The cost of the policy written for 24 hours was $7.13.

# # #

We drove through the border gate about noon on February 8. No formalities whatsoever — just a wave from the Mexican border guards and there we were on the other side of the chain link fence. Picked up Mexican Route 2 in Sonoita and headed west. The highway was fine — just two lanes, but perfectly adequate. It was dry, desolate country. The only traffic were Mexican trucks and an occasional bus. For quite a few miles, we skirted the chain link fence. Then the road wound into some mountains. I preferred those vistas. There were numerous shrines along the highway; memorials for someone who had had a fatal accident there. Some of them were quite ornate. All were decorated with colorful paper flowers. It was easy driving. Most of the truckers would wave. I didn't feel I was in a foreign land.

Westward Ho!

It was only 124 miles to San Luis where we again moved to the other side of the chain link fence. The most difficult part of the journey was locating the border crossing. When we did, I had to assure US customs that we had not stopped and picked up any contraband and that Ink had her vaccinations. The inspection didn't take long. We then rolled through farmland into Yuma. Pressed on to El Centro and stayed there for the night after a lovely day of Mexican travel.

# # #

The El Centro RV park was one which catered to Snow Birds. They seemed a little embarrassed by my small, unpretentious Tessie. Parked us right behind the kitchen on a concrete pad. Not much, but we only needed a place to sleep. Ink and I took a turn around the grounds. Noticed there were a lot of permanent trailers and a golf course. Not our usual fare, but it filled the need that night.

# # #

Got away early. Looked at the map and knew the Interstate would be the quickest, easiest way to get to Irvine. Didn't do that. Instead, we shunned pikes once again. Headed north to Brawley and took Route 78 through the Anza-Borrego desert. Nice country, but cold and windy. Climbed into the mountain communities of Julian and Romona, then dropped down to Escondido and into the crush of California traffic. We were in the midst of what seemed like a million cars. It was raining; a gloomy, gloomy day. Decided to press on to Irvine in spite of being tired and hating all the traffic. It was the kind of evening you longed to be with family.

Pulled into Irvine about 4:30 p.m. I had not called ahead — hadn't seen a pay phone in the mad jam of traffic. For that matter, I had no phone numbers for either Scot or Juli at work. Wound through the narrow streets of the development and found the kid's townhouse. They were walking their basset hound, Fred, and saw me. There I was — unannounced and uninvited — which did unsettle Juli a bit. I was sorry about that, but spent the night with them, happy to be out of the rain and the traffic.

We all recognized that Tessie was a hazard on the narrow streets in the area. So, the next day I made arrangements for space at Newport Dunes RV, just a short way from the kids.

Before going down to park up, I managed some overdue chores. Did marketing, stopped at our former veterinarian and got Ink a supply of heartworm pills, sent flowers to LaVerne in thanks for her hospitality, and mailed out postcards.

We had the park all to ourselves. No one there except some birds floating on the bay. Pulled up close to a restroom and away from the water. It was not swimming weather even for Ink. Popped up, plugged in, and cleaned Tessie, since the kids were coming for dinner.

Scot and Juli arrived laden with flowers, a huge chunk of brie, and lots of good cheer. It's tight quarters in Tessie for three people, but we had a passable meal and a great visit.

On Saturday, Scot rode down on his bike and had lunch with us. Saturday night we went to Balboa for dinner. Ink didn't mind staying and guarding the house. She was weary from chasing seagulls around the bay. The weather continued cold.

At dinner, the kids asked, "Well, where are you going, Mom?"

I said, "You know, I can't get warm. I haven't been warm since I left Tempe. I think I'm going to the Baja. Surely it'll be warmer there."

And, it was, "Go for it!"

I might have had doubts about tackling the Baja had I not

Westward Ho!

driven Tessie 14,000 miles on the Eastern portion of the trip. I had great faith in that little rig. The Baja seemed the logical place to escape the cold gripping the entire western United States that winter of 1989.

Sunday morning we drove over to Scot and Juli's for a hearty breakfast. Ink and Fred sniffed each other and settled down together. We ate and had our final visit. Called Pam and asked her to hold mail until she heard from me. Then Mark and Lois to let them know I was heading further south. And, after warm hugs and admonitions from Scot and Juli to be careful, we pulled back onto Interstate 5. Most cars were speeding past us. I enjoyed the play of turn signals winking and blinking like fire-flies as they wove in and out of six lanes of traffic.

Decided not to tackle the border crossing that evening. We stayed at a small campground in San Ysidero. En route to the RV park, spotted a sign advertising Mexican Insurance. I stopped and bought a month's policy, thinking that would give us ample time to explore the Baja Peninsula. Little did I know what that enchanted land had in store for Ink and me.

The campground was a subdued place, filled with campers who crossed the border for laetrile treatments for cancer. We took a short walk, then retreated to Tessie.

After dinner, I read my Mexican policy. It was issued by Aseguradora Cuauhtemoc, S. A. Written by Instant Mexico Auto Insurance for thirty days: 2/13/89 to 3/15/89. Here again, the only thing covered was liability. I took out a rider for emergency legal services which cost $24.30 for a total premium for one month of $119.09. I had this neat little booklet with emergency legal services phone numbers and a list of adjustors in case of an accident. It certainly gave me a feeling of confidence. I didn't know then that the policy was overpriced and outdated. But I learned.

Tackling the Transpeninsular

With the continuing synchronicity of this journey, I crossed the border on February 13, 1989 — three years to the day that my divorce was finalized. I certainly felt I had come a long way — both figuratively and literally.

We crossed into Tijuana for our tour of the Baja Peninsula, armed with a map, my camper guide and a lot of faith. Tijuana has a population of about a million people. I'm sure half of them were in cars trying to get across the border. It was a long wait. The Tijuana crossing is billed as the busiest in the world. When we were waved into Mexico, I found the other half million people racing cars and trucks around a traffic circle. I was caught up in a whirlpool of traffic — vehicles coming from all sides and not a directional sign in sight. Ink was on the bed looking a little concerned. I'm sure I heard her mutter, "Oh, my God, here we go again." Tessie eased along with her usual style and grace. We negotiated a few more wild traffic circles and presently I saw a sign for Ensenada. We were on our way south on the Transpeninsular Highway. I had no need to worry about road signs in the Baja. This highway is the only game in town; designated Route 1, it stretches from Tijuana to Cabo San Lucas and Land's End — a distance of 1065 miles.

We were on the expressway between Tijuana and Ensenada — a toll road. It was good, divided highway and easy driving. The vistas of the Pacific were magnificent. The trip that day cost $2.25 in tolls. In this area there was lots of development and lots of condo sales signs. An

Tackling the Transpeninsular

extension of California, U.S.A.

We stopped early at an American type resort in Las Salinas north of Ensenada. I didn't feel like tackling it the same day we did Tijuana. So the gypsy caravan pulled into this lush resort and made arrangements for space. The prices were lush, too — $20.00 per night. It was beautiful and had great amenities — right on the beach with tennis courts, pool and jacuzzi, store, laundry, and cantina. I did a load of wash. Ink came with me and no one minded my dog running free. Thought of eating in the cantina, but instead Ink and I strolled the beach at sunset. Saw no one. We had only the rumbling Pacific for company. It was cold enough to wear my down jacket. Ate dinner then headed for a hot shower.

I was reading when Ink fussed. Looked out and saw a handsome dog coming across the lot checking out the trash cans. Ink, of course, jumped out and frolicked with this animal for a while. I sat and watched the ocean. When we finally settled, Ink told me she thought she was going to like the Baja and all the freedom.

Thank God my camper guide had a section on Mexico. It was comforting to see there were campgrounds listed. Studied it for a while. Knew we had to get further south. The air was too cool here at Las Salinas.

# # #

Day two was tollway driving into Ensenada. The total toll from Tijuana to Ensenada was $3.60. A small price to pay for excellent roads and great scenery. I noticed highway signs which read: *No tira la busura.* Learned they meant don't throw trash. Mexico is becoming environmentally aware.

Ensenada was another big traffic jam: lots of construction and detours. We were routed through the main section of town and each street had a traffic signal or stop sign. The drivers were polite and would wave me into line with a smile. It's a beautiful city on the edge of the Pacific; Baja's third largest. And it's the largest seaport due to its position on Bahia de Todos Santos. Ensenada is close enough to the States to have fast food chains, but it still retains a certain foreign quality. We had an in-depth look while waiting for stop lights.

South of Ensenada, we drove though a fertile valley with vineyards, olive orchards, and fields of tomatoes. All this lush growth was supported by pipe irrigation. There were many small villages along the highway, so a lot of traffic. The road had narrowed to two lanes and I had to pay attention to driving.

I had read an ad for a campground at San Quentin called Cielito Lindo. Although it was not far, it seemed enough driving for one day in this foreign land. We passed a large tomato processing and shipping plant. Spied a small sign directing us to the right. Headed across the sand dunes and, sure enough, there was a camping place. A California couple in a big, yellow bus was running this park. There was no electricity and the water was not potable. But the setting was lovely and I gladly paid the $4.00 fee.

Ink and I walked over the dunes and were enthralled with the large orange seashells lying everywhere. That plus millions of Western Meadowlarks added to our pleasure. The California couple had a playful Lab. He and Ink patrolled the grounds together. Two female dogs who obviously had had recent litters came over timidly to watch Ink and the Lab. Lovely creatures, but very thin. We gave them some dinner. Next morning, they both brought out their puppies for us to admire. Each had three pups. We gave them a bite to eat, too. Ink thought it was great fun and frisked around with her new found friends. No language barrier between the dogs.

Sipped coffee, listened to the Meadowlarks, and watched the dog's antics. About 11 a.m. we pulled away from this delightful spot, grateful for the songs of the Meadowlarks and some better fed dogs.

Soon the fertile valley turned to desert. The road grew more narrow and rough, winding up and down the terrain of the land. These depressions would have been called arroyos in New Mexico. In the Baja they are called *"vados"*. Tessie could speed down them, but usually was in second gear before we reached the top. There were sharp curves, blind curves, cows, burros, horses, and goats on the highway. Not a road on which to speed; however, the scenery was so dazzling that I drove only about 40 mph. It was tiring, but never dull.

We turned inland about 20 miles south of San Quentin at El Rosario. This is spectacular Sonoran desert country — mountain ranges all around and no sign of human life. The area is called Las Virgenes, a region of spectacular rock formations and many varieties of cactus and other desert vegetation.

Made it to Catavina that evening. It's a small oasis in the interior. We stayed at one of the government-built *paradores*. These campgrounds were built when the Transpeninsular was completed in 1974. There were a couple of barracks-type buildings which housed the restrooms and showers. A big diesel generator provided electricity from 5 p.m. until 10 p.m. It was nice to use the toaster oven for dinner, but I was glad when that noisy generator turned off.

The campground setting at Catavina was fascinating. The grounds were filled with huge boulders and various cacti — the most spectacular being the organ pipe and the cardon which is a cousin to the saguaro and looks like it. We were parked right next to a tall boojum tree. The boojum or cirio is one of the most fascinating plants in the Baja. It grows in a region about 150 miles wide across the peninsula from El Rosario to just north of Guerrero Negro. It's a relative of the ocotillo and looks rather like an upside down carrot. As it grows skyward, it puts out spindly arms which seem to be waving madly. When it's young, it resembles a sweet potato, then as it gets older it's more like a carrot growing upside down — just this barren thorny stalk with curly flowering branches on the top at times, depending on the moisture. We walked and studied the various flora in this area. Visited with the other hardy souls in the park.

I settled Ink and went over to the barracks for a shower. This is when I learned a few precautions needed when traveling the Baja. As you entered the building, there were sinks to the right and toilet stalls to the left. Off a separate hallway, there were three shower stalls. Over the years, the water from the showers had rotted away the flooring and to get into the stalls, I had to skirt some gaping holes. Once in the shower, I discovered that "C" on the faucet does not necessarily mean cold. More often than not the "C" stands for *caliente* which is hot. I learned that night to always check out that stream of water before I stepped under it. And, the water, once I learned how to adjust the faucets, was hot. Jumped over the holes in the floor and decided I'd go to the toilet before heading back to Ink and Tessie. One more lesson learned: you are not to put toilet paper in the toilet. There's a box or a basket in which you place the toilet paper. Got back to the camper, cleaner and wiser on the ways of campgrounds in Baja.

There's a La Pinta Hotel and gasoline here in Catavina. The spot for those brave travelers who came this far south before the road was paved was Rancho Santa Ines, however. It's a short distance south to the left. There's still a small campground and a wonderful restaurant. It was

Tackling the Transpeninsular

here that the Transpeninsular was completed. Construction was from both north and south and connected here. A small plaque beside the highway notes this.

# # #

The 16th (our fourth day on the Transpeninsular) we were driving through inland desert. There was no traffic, just mountain peaks in the distance and New Mexico type scenery. The road was rough and narrow with numerous *vados*. Tessie sped down and chugged up, but kept humming. I noted, with some trepidation, that there were long stretches of highway with no shoulders. Thought fleetingly that if you had a problem, there was no way to pull off the road. Put that out of my mind as Tessie kept purring along.

We arrived at Guerrero Negro early, but decided to stop at another *parador* named the Benito Juarez just off the highway. Guerrero Negro sits astride the 28th parallel, the boundary for Northern and Southern Baja California (*Baja norte y Baja sur*). There's a large arch across the highway with an eagle perched on top. The main part of town is to the west. Weather here is usually cloudy and damp from the prevailing ocean breezes.

When I went into the office, there was a man from Nevada arguing with the clerk about his charges. It's sad so many Americans are sure they're going to be cheated. Stories circulated in the States always warn about the perils of Mexico. The Nevada man must had heard all of them. He kept going over the bill, not understanding the exchange rate. *El Señor* behind the desk kept telling him in halting English that it was correct. I listened to this impasse compounded by the language barrier for a while. I understood that, indeed, *El Señor* was correct. He couldn't speak much English, but he could add. Finally, with some misgiving, I said, "Señor, permítame a explicar, por *favor,"* and turned to the fuming American. I told him that the charges were correct and ran them out on a piece of paper. He studied the figures for a few minutes, then stormed out of the office without a word of apology.

El Señor was grateful for my help. I registered. The fee was $4.50 — the same as Catavina. I asked him about propane. He told me there was a plant just down the road, then gave me all kinds of literature on the area. We parted friends.

Before parking, we found the propane plant and had Tessie's nearly empty bottle filled. The propane plants, like the Pemex stations, are government owned and operated. Tessie's tank is a bear to get out of the compartment, but the lads were accommodating and efficient. They removed the tank easily, filled it, and had it back in place in no time. I paid less that $3.00 for a full tank of propane.

We parked up, popped up, and plugged in. Then, walked the grounds in a cold, damp wind. This *parador* was exactly the same as Catavina — large barracks type buildings with shower and bathroom facilities, each space with a concrete pad backed by a whitewashed wall containing plug-ins for electricity, and the ubiquitous generator providing power from 5 to 10 p.m.

Since there were few campgrounds, I met the same people who had been at Catavina. There was also a caravan parked up in a circle to the rear of the grounds. The wagon master was herding his charges around and warning them to be careful. I know I was quite a thorn in the wagon master's side. Here I was tooling along all by myself with no protection from *bandidos* and not at all worried. I realized caravans were not for me. They were all huddled together and never interacted with the local people.

Perhaps, if they had, they would have found them delightful, accommodating, and non-threatening.

Tackling the Transpeninsular

I stayed at Benito Juarez another day so that we could visit the whale refuge (*Parque Natural de la Ballena Gris*). Just south of town, a marker shaped like a whale pointed the way. It was a horrid road — rutted and rough — that went through a large salt reclamation operation. However, the whale markers showed the way as we bounced along slowly.

When we arrived at the Refuge, we paid an admission fee of $3.00. Parked Tessie on the side of a dirt lane, then Ink and I climbed a sand dune and wandered down to the bay. There were all kinds of sea and shore birds. Ink took a swim and I waded. We ate lunch sitting on the dunes watching whales cavorting in the bay. There were a few boats with whale-watchers out in the water. We found that the easy way to spot the whales in this vast lagoon was to watch those boats. In actuality, the whales were watching the tourists. They would come up close to the boats to stare at these creatures invading their territory.

We spent the afternoon enjoying whales and seabirds. It was awesome. Most Americans refer to this bay as Scammon's Lagoon after Charles Scammon who discovered it. He decimated most of the grey whale population with a massive slaughter of these magnificent animals. The estimated number of grey whales in 1937 was only 300, but they have made a remarkable recovery.

In fall, these fifty foot giants leave the Arctic and begin the longest migration of any mammal to their winter calving grounds here in Mexico. The babies are fifteen feet long and weigh 1000 pounds when born. They put on nearly 100 pounds of weight each day for several months before following their mothers back to the Arctic in the spring.

After a serendipitous afternoon, we headed back across the salt flats. I missed a turn somewhere and we wandered through miles of salt. Just kept creeping along and eventually we came to the highway. Everything was coated in a fine white shroud.

When we got back, I hosed Ink down and dried her well, then swept the salt silt out of Tessie. Had to rearrange a few things after the jarring drive. Finally, I had a hot shower. The floor in this barracks was in good shape — no jumping over gaping holes and the water was hot. Weather continued cool and windy, so we ate a quiet dinner inside. Turned in early looking forward to more adventures in Baja Sur.

# # #

Saturday morning, we did a turn around the grounds and visited a bit. The caravaners were all getting or being organized by the wagon master. Talked with a woman from Oregon. Their Ford broke down and they had been in the campground for two weeks. They were now negotiating to have the Ford towed to the border. I thought to myself, I surely hope Tess keeps purring. Refused to worry about a break down before it happened. Besides, being stranded in the Baja held a certain appeal for me.

We were on Route 1 by 10 a.m. heading southeast through the Vizcaino Desert and into the interior. This area receives less rainfall that any other region of the Baja and is always parched. There was nothing but *vados,* rugged mountains, and bleak country.

A German couple at Benito Juarez suggested I drive into San Ignacio and view the old mission church. After the arid scenery, the lush valley of Arroyo San Ignacio was a welcome surprise. Thousands of date palms blanketed the valley in a sea of green. This small town in the middle of the desert is a true oasis and blessed with an abundant underground water supply. We turned off the Trans-peninsular and drove west on a paved road past a large lake

Tackling the Transpeninsular

surrounded by palms, a La Pinta Hotel, and finally came to the plaza. It was shady and serene — ringed by large laurel trees and dominated by the old mission church built in 1728 by the Jesuits. Restored in 1976, it is used daily by the local citizens. It's one of the best preserved of the many missions in Baja with walls of four-foot thick quarried lava rock. The dates were also introduced by the Jesuits and continue to be the primary crop of San Ignacio.

More desert driving, then a steep, winding climb up the Sierra de Santa Lucia. On the down hill side, we caught our first glimpse of the Gulf of California glistening way below us. It was a treacherous descent and we took it slow and easy. Once down the mountain, the highway skirted the gulf. A few miles south, was the old mining town of Santa Rosalia founded when copper was discovered in the 1870's.

There are still remnants of the French mining operation. We wound past rusting machinery and some of the old smelter buildings as we drove into town. Turned off the highway once again and headed up a steep street to see the steel-fabricated church designed by Gustave Eiffel. The church was displayed at the St. Louis World's Fair and, somehow, ended up here in Santa Rosalia. I was surprised and delighted when I read the plaque — the church is named Santa Barbara.

Back on the Transpeninsular, we passed the ferry terminus for the boats to Guaymas and the mainland, a Pemex station, and a new lovely *malecón* (seaside park).

Continued south along that incredible blue gulf, arriving in Mulege about 3:30 p.m. on a Saturday. It was packed with tourists, but I did a turn around the main section of town. I needed supplies and was getting short of money; however, I didn't see anything promising and retreated to the highway.

Mulege is a popular tourist destination. It's another oasis

with numerous palms and tropical plants. It has a river — the Santa Rosalia. Mission Santa Rosalia de Mulege has one of the loveliest settings of all the missions. Mulege is also the locale of the old prison. Before the road was built, the prisoners were free to leave the prison during the day and return in the evening. No one worried about them escaping — there was nowhere to go in this remote region. All that has changed. The old prison is now a museum and there's a high security prison south of Santa Rosalla.

We checked out Hotel Serenadad, the venerable old inn that had been there before the road was paved. It lured fishermen from all over the world with the great Gulf fishing and a landing strip for small private planes. There was a campground now — right on the tarmac. It was too crowded for us. Drove back up the highway looking for a more spacious, quiet spot. Noticed a sign for the Maria Isabel RV Park. Scooted down the hill and found a lovely place close to the river. The owner had a small bakery and his home-baked wares were delicious. He suggested I park up by the bar-b-que, not plug in, and charged me $3.00 a night. We had the heavenly smells from the bakery and some grass for Ink to relax on.

Got popped up, then strolled down to the river. It was cool and lush, lots of birds and lots of tropical plants. Ink had a swim. There were small villas along the river here in the park. Each had space to park a camper. I asked Daniel, the owner, about them. Found they were for sale for around 11 to 15 thousand dollars. We had a quiet dinner and settled in early to the sounds of guitars playing and dogs barking.

# # #

Decided to spend Sunday here in this peaceful setting. There was no way to get money. Mulege had no full service bank. Some kind Canadians told me the nearest bank was in Loretto. So we stayed and had a restful day. The restrooms were luxurious after two nights in the *paradores*. The people were friendly and the grounds pleasant.

The shelf in the closet was loose again and I fixed it. Maribel, the owner's wife, stopped to visit. She loved Ink and offered to take her anytime I wanted to be rid of her. She understood when I said I thought I could part with an arm easier than with Ink. We all sat on the grass and enjoyed the warm, tropical weather. I was finally beginning to thaw.

# # #

Monday morning, decided to take a chance with supplies further south rather than dealing with Mulege's narrow streets. Maribel stopped with some warm muffins that she insisted I take. She and Ink had their good-bye pats and kisses. We left the campground about 10 a.m. with no cigarettes, very little money, and not much gasoline for the eighty mile drive to Loretto.

This is some of the most beautiful scenery in all the Baja. Driving along the shores of Bahia Concepcion with the vivid blue waters of the Gulf contrasting sharply with the pristine white beaches almost took my mind off our precarious gas supply. We made it into the Pemex station in Loretto by the gulp of the tank. My bill was 31,000 pesos and all I had was 27,000 pesos. The station attendant smiled and waved me on my way with, "It's okay, lady." Thank God for small kindnesses.

Next was finding a bank. I walked into Bancomer and managed a cash advance. The exchange rate was 3500 pesos to the dollar. It was 12:45 p.m. I noted that the bank closed for the day at 1:00 p.m. — as do all banks in Mexico. Realized my guides were still taking care of me.

Loretto is the oldest settlement in Baja California. It, at

one time, was the capital of all the California Territory which extended as far north as San Francisco. The old mission church has been restored and is an imposing edifice towering over a shady and inviting plaza. There's an interesting museum adjoining the church.

Got directions to campgrounds which were south of town on the beach. There were two side by side. One had the caravan parked out in the sun and sand, the other was ringed with palms and looked much more inviting. We parked in the shady, palm ringed park. It was run by a Mexican couple with two darling children. I made arrangements for our space, then drove back into town to the Mercado for supplies. It was siesta time and the store was uncrowded, so I browsed since I now had *mucho dinero*. There was an adequate supply of food plus cook ware, clothing, and sundries. I bought food, a great straw hat, and a pair of cotton shorts.

We were back at the campground by 4 p.m. Ink and I took a walk on the beach — I needed an excuse to try my new straw hat. We wandered for a few miles, wading in the warm waters, and enjoying the scenery.

Had just gotten back to Tessie when a man came through the grounds selling fresh scallops. I bought half a kilo (about a pound) for 8,000 pesos. Had a sumptuous scallop dinner and ate the whole pound. Took a turn around the nearly empty grounds at sunset. Sat on the back wall looking at the islands in the Gulf fading into the darkness. Enjoyed a romantic moon shining through the palms. Turned in feeling all was well in my world here in the Baja.

# # #

It was such a lovely spot that we stayed at Las Palmas Tuesday. Took a long, long walk. The beach was rocky, and shelling not too good, but the islands off the coast were

Tackling the Transpeninsular

spectacular. As we were returning, a few of the caravaners waved to me and seemed surprised that I was still just fine. Some were complaining that they needed shade. Indeed, they were at the full mercy of the sun. Evidently when you're traveling with a caravan, you have no control over where you park. Ink and I returned to our palm shaded site, thankful that we could make our own decisions.

There was an international group, small tho' it was, in the park: a couple from Edmonton, Canada, another couple from Anchorage, and three fishermen from Costa Mesa, California.

I had noticed a washer and dryer in the lobby and decided to do a load of laundry. I started to put the clothes in the dryer and learned it was not hooked up so I hung wet clothes on a line strung around the palm trees. Always ask lots of questions in Mexico. No one offers any information unless you ask. The couple just smiled and said, of course I could use the laundry facilities, but did not mention the dryer was inoperable. No big problem. I sat and visited with people as they strolled by my laundry-beladen site. And more vendors — selling shells, tamales, and more scallops. No need to go to market, the market comes to you. It was a lovely day, in a lovely setting, with lovely people.

# # #

Wednesday, we got an early start. I had noticed an interesting boutique on the way to the campground and wanted to stop. It was delightful and I bought some great Mexican cotton clothes. Parked Tessie in the shade and dashed up to the plaza for a few photos. We pulled onto the Transpeninsular about noon.

The road south of Loretto was horrendous — pot holes so numerous there was no way to miss them; however, the scenery was spectacular, so it all balanced out. We drove very slowly and gazed at Isla Carmen floating in the sea, white beaches beckoning, and the Sierra de la Giganta towering above us to the west. There were campers parked here and there on those inviting beaches. It is one of the beauties of the Baja; many beaches are free and you can park wherever the mood strikes you. Much as I felt like pulling over, we kept bouncing along.

The Mexican government has an ambitious project underway south of Loretto in Nopolo. They have built a grand hotel. The golf course has large houses ringing it. The airport is operable and they are hoping to lure tourists to the area. I pulled off the rough highway and drove around. There was no sign of activity, but many houses under construction. No people in sight so we took a short walk. I needed to rest my aching arms. Then, it was back to the jarring road, gritting my teeth, and clinching the steering wheel.

We passed signs for Juncalito, Puerto Escondido, and Ligui — all great Gulf beaches. Then started the ascent of the Sierra de la Giganta. It's a rough, twisty, first-gear climb before breaking out onto the Magdalena Plain. This high inland country is now being farmed. Villa Insurgentes and Ciudad Constitucion are both centers of the new agriculture in the area. Lots of traffic and lots of chemical fertilizer plants. After these cities, the highway stretches across the plain.

At El Cien, so named because it is 100 kilometers from La Paz, the road improves and the vegetation becomes more dense. There were more cows, horses, and burros on the highway than cars. I never knew what would be around the next curve, so I did pay attention.

At a point near the K34 marker, there's a white shrine on the west side of the road. There was room to park, Ink and I both needed to stretch, so we pulled in. Hiked up a trail

Tackling the Transpeninsular

for some distance. From this high point, if you look carefully, you can see both the Pacific and the Gulf. From here, it's down-hill all the way to La Paz.

With a population of 100,000, La Paz is the largest city in Baja Sur. It's charming and cosmopolitan. We spent the night in a brand new park on the Bay. The caravan was there, plus lots of other people I had seen on the trek down the peninsula. We all greeted and had a good visit. A few appeared incredulous that I was still fine; going strong and having no problems, traveling alone and loving it.

As I was setting up, a handsome lad came by taking orders for dinner at the small restaurant. I thought, why not? So, I ordered enchiladas for 7:30 p.m.

Ink had a romp with the campground puppy. I showered and shampooed in the nicest restroom since our first day in the Baja. It, too, had a basket beside the toilet for paper. Seemed to be the custom. Dressed in my Loretto pant suit and wandered down to the cantina where Alberto, the lad who had taken my order, greeted me with, "You look very well." I felt very well.

Had a delightful dinner and a small celebration for having made it safely to La Paz. The food was very good and the service was even better. I had three waiters hovering over me at all times. Ah, Mexico.

# # #

Next morning, at the suggestion of more Canadians, I stopped at a super supermarket. The CCC (Central Commercial Californiano) had everything. Found Purina dog chow and Ken-L-Ration, film, quinine, great seafood, and fresh fruits and vegetables. Stocked up and enjoyed that huge market and the prices. Then, it was downtown for another cash advance at Bancomer. Traffic was heavy. I pulled straight into the curb in front of the bank. No problem getting *dinero,* but I could not see to pull out of the space into traffic. A man in a brown uniform stopped all traffic until I backed out.

Got hopelessly lost trying to find Route 1 heading south out of this fair city. Kept going in circles. It felt like Moncton re-visited. Eventually, after having a thorough look at La Paz, we stumbled onto Route 1 and headed for Cabo San Lucas and Land's End. (Finisterra).

It was hot inland driving; up and down *vados,* livestock on the roadway, and slow going. Came back to the sea at San Jose del Cabo. This area had lots of condos and even a Howard Johnson with a golf course. Kept rolling and arrived at a quaint RV park on the outskirts of Cabo about 4:30 p.m. on Thursday, February 23, 1989. We were now as far south as Tessie could take us unless we put pontoons on her.

The campground, the Cabo Cielo, catered to fishermen. It was pleasant and tropical. From Tessie's doorway, we had an unfettered view of Los Arcos — the imposing rock formation at the juncture of the Gulf of California and the Pacific. It was beautiful. I thanked my gods and guides for a glorious, but strenuous trip down this magnificent peninsula. We had made it.

#

Ink and I awoke to sunshine and birds twittering that Friday morning. I glanced out at the bay. There was a ferry boat steaming toward the mainland. Learned it was the ferry to Puerto Vallarta. Decided it was a day to rest on our laurels. We had now driven from the tip of Cape Briton to the tip of Baja. The journey had been a glorious adventure and Tessie had carried us safely and well. A few non-driving days seemed in order. There was good hiking and the grounds were spacious. This was a place to stay and rest a bit.

I tightened all the screws in the camper, did a visual

Tackling the Transpeninsular 47

inspection of the underside, and checked oil, water, and belts under the hood. Then, it was into the storage bins under the seats to change out clothing. Put all the woolens away and was delighted with that project. Got out shorts and hoped not to see wool again for some time.

Ink noticed the mid-day heat. She curled up under Tessie and was content not to have to help with driving. About three in the afternoon, we strolled over to sit in the large *palapa* on the grounds. A *palapa* is a thatched roofed circular structure sometimes with walls and sometimes without. This one had no walls and an unencumbered view of the bay. There was no one there, so Ink sprawled on the cool tile floor, and I settled down at one of the little tables. We enjoyed the coolness and the view.

I asked Luis, the lad who ran the park, about getting to the beach. He pointed down a dirt road beside the campground and said to follow it. Around five, when it had cooled, Ink and I set off down the road. About a quarter of a mile into our quest for the sea, we came to a cemetery. It was surrounded by an ornate wrought-iron fence. There were many mausoleums and shrines. Each grave site was gaily decorated with paper flowers.

We skirted the cemetery and hiked on through lush vegetation. Were climbing up a rutted road when we came to a barbed wire fence. I hesitated for a minute, but Ink had already gone underneath it. So I did, too. We climbed further and broke out on a ridge above the Gulf with yet another fence. We went under that one, too. Then slid down the sand dunes to an incredible beach with magnificent views of the Arches. Ink swam, I waded and gathered seashells. That stroll was worth the whole trip. Climbed back up the hill. Then sat and feasted on the view, as I gave thanks to my gods and guides for a safe journey. Needless to say, there was no one around. I still have no idea if we were trespassing.

When we got back to camp, a group of *Norteamericanos* stopped to say they were leaving for the States. The two couples were traveling in a Tioga. One lady and I had chatted before. She told me they had rented three-wheel trykes in Cabo and her woman friend had taken a nasty spill. She was cut up and unconscious. She had been taken to the hospital, but they now had her loaded in the camper. They were planning to leave right away. It seemed a bad time to be tackling that long trip. I wished them safe journeying and cautioned them to be careful. I had a fleeting thought that if something should happen to me, what or who would take care of my Ink? Gave my girl a hug and promised to be careful.

I had really stocked up on produce at CCC. That evening I stuffed a papaya with tuna salad. Had a *bolillo* — the wonderful crusty Mexican rolls. All this out at the picnic table gazing at the bay. The sun had set and it was cool and pleasant.

Got Ink settled, went for a shower, then into bed. Woke in the night to hear waves pounding on the shore; slow, steady, and powerful — the heartbeat of the world. Lay there happy to be at Land's End. Said a small prayer for the couples on their way up the Baja with the injured woman.

# # #

Sun was flooding into the camper when we woke on Saturday morning. Ink and I did a round of the grounds. I then made an executive decision. Went over and paid Luis for two more nights. This seemed a good place to stay and rest. The price was right — $4.50 a night.

In the heat of the day, we retreated to the *palapa* — still no one there. Most of the campers had air-conditioning and stayed inside. A lady had given me the Wednesday *Los*

Tackling the Transpeninsular

Angeles Times. I glanced briefly at all the gory, dreary news and decided I didn't need it. Worked on a vest I was knitting for Pam. Enjoyed the sea breeze drifting through the *palapa.*

Ink and I headed past the cemetery and through the fences to the beach a little before sunset. Again, we frolicked alone. Got home and had dinner at the picnic table. Took a shower and turned in. The sounds of Saturday night revelry — guitars and barking dogs — were drifting across the bay as we went to sleep.

# # #

Sunday, we decided to check out the town of Cabo San Lucas. Secured the top and drove on down the highway. Found a Pemex station about a mile from the campground and pulled in. Buying gasoline in Mexico is a social event. Three smiling lads were beside the camper in a minute. One took the keys and started to fill the tank, one washed the windshield, and the other proposed. It's usually this way and it's fun. The Mexicans have a great sense of humor.

Proceeded on down the main street which was torn up. There was construction underway, so we had to weave from one side of the divided highway to the other. Kept weaving past big hotels and rental places for bikes, surf boards, and boats. There were lots of shops and restaurants. Cabo is a tourist town and shows it. Drove past more hotels and condos and out a two-lane road to the quay on the harbor. No ferry boat this morning, but some great sailing ships anchored in the snug harbor. We parked and watched the boats bobbing gently, and the pelicans and seagulls circling. Then on around the quay and back into town.

Passed a bustling open-air bazaar next to the bay with a big parking lot. I couldn't resist it. Promised Ink I would not take long. Left her to guard the house and did a quick turn around the various stalls. There were all kinds of tourist enticements: jewelry, onyx carvings, clothing, sombreros, and lots of pottery. No post cards anywhere, however. Would have bought some cards. Not finding any, I went back to Ink and Tessie.

We toured downtown and fought the battle of narrow, congested streets. Everyone was friendly and laid-back and I had no problem with the traffic. Kept looking for the post office, but struck out there, too. In driving around, we noticed a road sign for Route 19 heading north up the Pacific coast and connecting with the Transpeninsular just south of La Paz. Looked like an inviting way to go. Before Route 19 was completed, the only way back north was the same Route 1. Since I have always hated going the same way twice, was delighted to see an alternative, short though it was.

Back at Cabo Cielo, there was no one around. Ink and I staked out our spot in the *palapa*. I finished Pam's vest. Took our rounds at sunset, had dinner, then to bed early. Tomorrow, we would meander north on the Pacific side after a relaxing and replenishing stay at Finisterra.

The Beach

Monday, February 27, we headed round the tip of the peninsula and north on Route 19. I was half way through my thirty days of insurance, so felt we were on schedule.

It was a long climb out of Cabo past new developments growing up the hill. I could see the harbor in the rear view mirror. Soon we were on a high plain above the sea. We were rolling up and down the *vados* with the Pacific in view to the west. There were quiet coves, white sand, and that vast ocean out there. I said to Ink, "Now, this is how I pictured Baja. I think we ought to head down one of those rutty roads and stake out a claim." But, we kept driving. The highway was good. There was no traffic, no sign of people, just a few herds of goats, some cattle, and lots of *vados*.

Passed through the village of Elias Calles. Not much there, just fertile fields and a small school house. After a sweeping curve in the road, we came onto a glorious vista of the sea and those white beaches. We had just cleared another *vado* and were rolling along a few miles south of Pescadero. I passed a small green sign on the crest of a hill reading: RV Trailer Park. Was beyond it by the time it registered, but turned around and went back to see about it.

We were bouncing down a rough, dirt road when a car with Washington state plates passed us. There were two couples and they all waved. Kept jouncing along and came to the Washington car stopped on the road. The two gals came back to the camper and urged me not to give up, just keep jolting along. They gave me directions to the RV park and informed me that there was a single woman from Santa Fe camped there. They couldn't know that the gypsy caravan never gave up, but I enjoyed the encouragement.

When we, at last, came to the fork in the road, I heeded directions and turned left. But not before we took in the view. Spread before us was a pristine beach sheltered on the north by a granite outcropping and stretching away to the south in a crescent. There were remnants of a *parador*. Beyond a chain link fence we could see three trailers parked up.

Drove through the park and out to a welcoming committee on the beach. Ardis and John, Ann and Bob, and El, the gal from Santa Fe were lined up waiting for me. I parked a bit to the west of the group, then went over to warm welcomes from all of them. We chatted for a while, then Ink I headed out for a little exploration.

This was the spot I had been looking for in Baja; a perfect melding of sea, desert, and mountains. A four mile crescent of hard sand beaches, the Pacific, whales, frigate birds, brown pelicans, California quail, cactus wrens, mocking birds, flickers, and scads of sparrows. The dunes were covered with desert wild flowers. It was a mystical, magical place full of energy and beauty. We certainly had seen our share of beaches, but Cerritos was "the beach." As Ink and I strolled along the shore I knew we had found a perfect spot for mind, soul, and body.

When we returned to Tessie, the group invited us to join them by the fire after dinner. The Washington couples were going to start back north soon. They lived on boats in Washington in the summer and then came to Baja in trailers in the winter months. El had trailered her Airstream down the peninsula from Santa Fe where she bought it.

Although she had lived in Santa Fe for two years, she was from New Hampshire originally.

Francisco, the caretaker for the campground, arrived and I made arrangements with him to spend five nights. I was worried about my insurance coverage and didn't think I could tarry longer than five days and get back to the border before it expired. However, this mystical place worked its magic on me and my plans changed radically.

We slept that night deeply and well with the Pacific rolling just outside our door. We had found "paradise."

# # #

I settled in like I was home. The four mile crescent of sand and surf, the Sonoran Desert vegetation, the mountains to the east, and the Pacific to the west made it a perfect spot. Ink and I agreed it was better that Padre Island National Seashore.

It was a place that spoke to me. Ink and I found an area down the beach on a high cliff overlooking the ocean. The land dropped off precipitously and I could watch the breakers change color — blues, greens, and every hue in between. I would sit there with the mountains behind me, the ocean spreading out before me, and feel a part of all that is. A part of the wisdom of the universe. No thought of linear time. Just this at-oneness with the world and everything in it. So at peace and so filled with joy. This was, indeed, a magical, mystical beach.

# # #

It certainly wasn't the amenities of the RV park that held us here. There was no electricity, no drinking water, and the *baños* had cold water showers. But I knew this beach was a special place for me.

I learned that this *parador* was on *ejido* land owned by the village of Pescadero. *Ejidos* are a communal form of government. The land is held in common by all members of the *ejido*. They came into being with the Constitution of 1917 as a way of restoring land to the Indians which had been taken during Spanish colonization by the large ranchers.

This particular *parador* had been hit hard by a hurricane. The roofs were off the barracks-style buildings. No one seemed prone to fix them. The concrete *baños* were operable, using water stored in *pilas* (cisterns) on top of the roof to flush the toilets and furnish shower water. There was a large storage *pila* which was filled by a water truck from Pescadero. It was lined in concrete and surrounded by a concrete platform. When you needed water, you removed the lid over an opening in the large cistern. Then you threw a bucket tied with a long rope into the water, let it float around until it was full, and pulled it up. If the water truck had filled the *pila* recently, the tug on the bucket was short and easy. If the water level was low, it was long and hard. Hefting that bucket of water was great for the arm muscles. The dogs drank this water with no ill effects and we showered in it. But, for drinking water, it was necessary to make a trip to the plaza in Pescadero or on into Todos Santos to fill water bottles. There was a grand Rolls-Royce diesel rusting away in the shed behind the *pila*.

None of these inconveniences mattered to me when compared to the beauty of the setting. The whales were on their northern trek after calving in the warm Baja waters. They did not come close to shore on the northern journey, but spouts were visible on the horizon.

I would sit and sip my coffee in the morning looking down the mist-shrouded beach at the mountains. In gazing at them, I noticed that, rather than the usual phallic symbolism so prevalent in nature, these were womanly mountains. I could discern a reclining female figure, legs spread and pregnant. There were breasts jutting into the

The Beach

sky everywhere. I named one fascinating formation the great vagina. From the other window, I could watch the waves foam up and around the rugged outcropping to the north. Usually, there was the call of a flicker and mockingbirds singing joyously. And, always, the steady beating of the waves on the shore.

# # #

The Washington couples hooked up trailers and left the beach about noon on Thursday. They planned to drive over to La Paz that day. Then they would make the long trip north at their leisure. I knew these caring people were relieved that someone was with El. We all had a last round of hugs and good wishes for a safe journey. Waved them away and El and I were left with the beach and grounds and each other.

We hit it off very well. El was a New England woman who had come to Santa Fe after the end of a 27 year marriage and six children. A Jungian psychologist, a devotee of the Sai Babba, and a much more soul-oriented person than I. She took me under her wing and showed me the ways of the Baja. She had been at Cerritos since December. Our conversations were always meaningful and enlightening — an exchange of different world-views, which both of us were able to discuss, contemplate, and accept. This makes for good conversation and good friendship. EL had a standard white poodle named Gilda who was much more aloof than my bouncy Ink, but they got along well, too. All in all a serendipitous setting.

# # #

On Friday, we had driven into Todos Santos in El's pickup. We were eating tacos at Pilar's Fish Taco Stand when El asked, "Barb, why don't you just stay here for a month?" That question brought into the open what my inner voice had been saying. I intuitively knew Cerritos was right. It was where I needed to be. I grinned at El and said, "Why not?" The die was cast. I would stay a while longer in this enchanting area. How lovely to be able to accept that inner guidance and not question! The beach was my spot and I had the wisdom to acknowledge it.

# # #

Saturday, it was back to Todos Santos to call the kids and let them know of my decision to tarry longer on this beach. Again, it was Pilar's. She had the only outside phone connection. You paid Pilar and she called through to the Mexican operator in La Paz who connected you with an operator in the States. It worked well except on Sundays when getting a Mexican operator was impossible. Pilar's was also the bus stop, so the little taco stand was a hub of the community. Pilar was a handsome, strong Mexican woman who was vital to the town of Todos Santos.

I had misgivings about letting Mark and Lois know of my decision. I should have known better. As always, it was, "Go for it, Mom." Mark said he was relieved that I was staying in one spot for a while. Pamie assured me she would forward mail to General Delivery once a month. What wonderful support and what an affirmation that I should stay right here.

# # #

The General Delivery system at the small post office in Todos Santos was unique. Mail was to be sent to: *Lista de Correos*. At that time, it was placed on the counter in a stack. You had to look though all of it to see if you had a letter. El told me that one letter, which we saw each time, had been there since she arrived in December. Still, the mail did come through. It usually took two weeks for delivery from the States, but we got our mail.

# # #

I had to work out costs with Francisco for a five week

stay. He told me that his *jefe,* Manuel, was to come from La Paz on Sunday and I should talk with him. Sure enough, Sunday about noon a bus pulled into the campground. It was Manuel and his family. El informed me that he had sired 23 children by nine different women.

Manuel was one smooth operator. He put the price of my five weeks to me with the kicker that Francisco would get some of the money. I was more than willing to see Francisco get paid, since Manuel rarely did that. We agreed on a price that was too high, but I was happy with it. Francisco would have money to feed his family. Manuel, in his effusive style, shook my hand and told me that I was free to stay at Cerritos for a year. I smiled and told him that I planned to check with Francisco to see that he got his money.

# # #

Strange, wonderful things happened at this beach. El and I had been talking about my problem of having to take the table down in Tessie and constantly having to re-arrange everything each day. We agreed that what I needed was a table and some chairs that I could put outside. Then I could leave the bed made up in Tess.

The next morning, I was walking to the *baño* and there by the chain-link fence were tables and a stack of chairs. Just ask and you shall receive. They had been brought in by Francisco for Manuel's family, of course. Still, there they were — just what I needed.

Asked Francisco about using a table and some chairs and he brought them over to Tessie. We set up a hospitality center on the south side of the camper out of the wind. It became the meeting and greeting place and was wonderful.

# # #

The campground dog, whom I named Madrita, decided she had a home with us. She was a gentle, well-mannered animal. In Baja, female dogs are not in demand. They're usually tossed out at an early age to fend for themselves. Some find refuge, as did Madrita, others die. This canny survivor would arrive each evening for dinner. We didn't mind feeding her. She was a good companion for Ink and I enjoyed her company, too. During the tourist season, she wondered from RV to RV and everyone gave her a handout. In the off season, she had trouble finding enough food, but somehow managed. Now that we were there, she was at ease and stayed close to Tessie. Usually slept at night under the camper in a hole she would dig out and get just right.

# # #

The welcome addition of table and chairs prompted me to build a fire pit. No problem with the pit since Ink and Madrita had dug out a big hole. I wandered the beach and picked up ocean-washed stones. Lugged them home in a bucket to line the pit. Then ringed the whole thing with abalone shells. There were few shells on the beach this time of year, but the stones that washed in were smooth and lovely. While choosing just the right ones, I spotted a big Ironwood log way down the beach. It looked like one of Picasso's wounded horses lying there on its side in the sand. I somehow tugged that *caballo* home. Ironwood is aptly named and is horribly heavy. But I knew I had to have that log by the fire pit. It was slow going and hard work. Eventually I got the log positioned where I wanted it.

That evening El and I sat on *caballo* by the fire and sipped Martinelli's sparkling cider. The sea was singing her soothing song, the stars were close enough to pluck from the sky. Who could ask for more?

# # #

Life on the beach evolved into a laid-back round of

walking, swimming, playing with the dogs, and enjoying this close tie with mother nature. There were the chores — pulling water from the cistern, trips for food, things to hold mind and body together; however, it was a satisfying routine and I thrived on it. El and I were both private women and some days we didn't even see each other, but knew we were there together.

# # #

I awoke one morning and knew I didn't want to see or talk to anyone on that glorious day. Packed a small lunch, some water, the camera and binoculars and asked Ink if she'd like to walk down the beach to the south outcropping. Of course, Ink was all for it. Had not left the parameters of the campground until Madrita joined us. The three of us headed south for a hike to the cove. I had not bothered to wear shoes nor to carry extra water for the dogs.

The aloe vera was in bloom — brilliant spikes of orange and gold covering the fields. We took pictures and kept ambling south. Got to the cove in three hours. The distance was farther than it looked. Ink and Madrita would wade in and out of the surf. I joined them at times since my feet were starting to hurt. The hard sand was quite abrasive. Got to that big outcropping sheltering a picturesque cove of white, white sand, huge black lava boulders, and the Pacific pounding in. It was worth the walk. We all sat and shared our small lunch then stretched out in the shade of the cliffs. Rested listening to the waves and the calls of gulls. We could have been alone on the planet.

Hated to leave this idyllic spot, but knew it was a long way back up the beach to the campground. Away we went, me and my two black companions. We made it back in about two and a half hours; hot and tired. The dogs were very thirsty. They drank long and hard then settled under Tessie in the shade. I sat down and put lotion on my burning feet.

El came down asking where we had been. When I told her of our hike, she informed me that the distance to the cove and back was about five miles. My feet knew they had hit that sand for five miles and my legs were fried, but what a great walk! Did not see a soul nor did I want to.

# # #

Women were constantly pulling into the campground. Perhaps it was the womanly mountains. They seemed to be led to Cerritos. These were women of substance — traveling alone. I met more women traveling solo in Baja than anywhere else on my journey. We all felt safe in spite of the lurid tales of *bandidos* and bad happenings that constantly circulated in the States.

All had tales to tell. Whereas, men talk in fact and information, we women converse in feeling and emotion. Evenings around a campfire were full of tales of bad relationships, hard times, and lots of sorrow. Some of the conversations would have made any man's hair stand on end. We enjoyed the camaraderie, the close encounters, and the catharsis of letting it all hang out.

One evening El stopped us cold with the comment that we had been talking for over an hour on vehicle maintenance and rig performance. This is of vital concern to those of us who travel alone. But, as El pointed out, we sounded like a bunch of truck drivers. Most of the women drove small vehicles. Many had Toyotas. One of the gals in a Toyota pickup with a small camper shell was talking away one night. She said, "Those 'pig rigs' never should come down the Baja." She meant, of course, the huge rigs with a car towed behind and all amenities of home. Truly, the roads in Baja do not lend themselves to big rigs. However, we all must travel in our own style. We women shunned the "pig rigs". With no electricity, water, or dump station, Cerritos did not attract many of them.

I remember one gal vividly. She drove in slowly one evening in a car. Parked under a tree inside the fence not far from Tessie. This woman's husband had left her six years before for some sweet, young thing. She was still grieving about it. She had no money, but was constantly dropping names and letting us know she had been quite wealthy. This didn't matter to either El or me, but we let her ramble.

I fed her each evening. Even though her monologue was tiresome, I couldn't let the poor thing starve. I'd hand a plate over the fence at dinnertime. The dogs and I came back from a morning stroll and the car was gone. She had been parked for three days. Asked Francisco if she had paid him, and, no, she had not. As Francisco put it, *"No tiene dinero."* I learned money isn't all that necessary if you choose your parking places carefully.

# # #

Pescadero was the nearest village. It was about six *kilometros* from the beach to the center of that bougainvillea-laden, little town. El and I went there often to fill water jugs in the plaza. All villages must provide water in the plazas for anyone's use. There was a grade school, the municipal building, a few small *tiendas,* some bars, and a baseball stadium. We came to know many of the people of the village. They were outgoing, cordial, and interested in any *gringas* passing through.

Bell was the official town greeter; an older man with great charm and a hearty laugh. He was stocky, with a shock of white hair usually covered with a straw sombrero. His favorite T-shirt sported a panda bear. We visited Ball's house one evening to meet some newly arrived *Norteamericanos* he had taken in. This was the attitude of all in Pescadero.

The Pescaderans were willing to provide shelter and help to anyone so long as they gave something in return. The few gringos living there found meaningful ways to contribute. The natives were delighted to have their children learn skills of any kind. One couple was provided with a house in return for ballet lessons for the young girls. Another twosome, Adam and Suzie, had arrived from Washington state with $5.00 in their pockets. Bell took them in. Suzie was a massage therapist, Adam could fix anything and they were contributing. We became good friends.

Adam took on the job of Tessie's maintenance. At that time, no Pemex station had facilities for changing oil. You bought the oil and did it yourself. Or, drove to a full-service garage in La Paz. I relied on Adam's expertise. He assured me Tessie was one fine machine and we'd try to keep her that way.

The evening we stopped at Bell's, he had just taken in another gringo. Roberto had been a hair stylist in Hollywood. He was going to live in Pescadero, set up a small salon, and teach some of the young women how to cut hair.

This was not a cash economy. There just wasn't much money, but the bartering system was alive and well. Suzie and Adam acquired all kinds of chickens, fruits, vegetables, and fish from the grateful people they helped. They eased into the slow routine of the village, saying they had found a home.

# # #

For a while, we had a Canadian lad living on the beach down from the campground. He was a tall, thin, gentle lad who had ridden a bicycle from British Columbia the entire length of the U.S. and Baja. He came to the beach with nothing more than a guitar, a tent, a few belongings and his bike. He would stop and visit some mornings on his way to Pescadero where he schooled children in guitar. The Pescaderans kept him well supplied with food. I recall a conversation we had over coffee at Tessie one morning. This dear lad asked, "Why couldn't they print all the bad news on page 13 of the papers and have the rest be happy news?" I loved the idea. The Pescaderans offered this lad a place to live, but one day he went his solitary way on his bike.

# # #

Then, there was the Christian missionary from the States who came to Pescadero with a van full of beans. Rather like bringing coals to Newcastle, you know. This man petitioned for land on which to build an orphanage. The people pointed out that there were no orphans in Pescadero. Someone would always take in another child and care for him as their own. He then tried for land for an old peoples' home and, again, the Pescaderans said that the old lived with their families until they died. The *ejido* met to discuss this minister's request. They turned him down flat. So far as I know, he took his beans back to the States with him.

# # #

The men of Pescadero were fishermen. They set out each morning in their tiny *pangas* from Punta Lobos. I would watch those small two-men boats heading south each morning and marvel at the courage of the crews. The *pangas* looked so tiny, bobbing on that vast ocean, but they were out there most days. They all belonged to a cooperative that had about 30 boats on the beach at Punta Lobos. The Mexican government subsidizes the purchase of the outboard motors and the boats. The men net the fish and store the catch in a center compartment of the *panga*. The beach is closed to any other boats.

The fun part is being there when the pangas return at the

end of the day. This site, like most along the Pacific side of southern Baja, has very steep drop-offs into the sea. The boats come in around three or four in the afternoon. They circle at the edge of a large lava outcropping about 100 yards off-shore, then catch a large wave, rev up the outboards, and ride those little *pangas* right up onto the beach. I'm sure the men could make a fortune selling rides to tourists; however, they're more interested in fishing.

Once the *pangas* are beached, the family arrives and the catch is sorted into piles: sierra, bonita, yellow-fin, red snapper, shark, dolfin-fish, and whatever else the sea provides. The fish are gutted and cleaned right there on the beach. Some of the debris is thrown out to the pelicans, some is thrown to all the stray dogs who congregate. Then the catch is loaded by species into plastic cartons, put into a large pickup, and taken to La Paz for sale.

The *co-operativa* cannot sell fish there at Punta Lobos, but a smiling fisherman sometimes offers one free of charge. These men brave that vast ocean each day and still are joyous and generous.

A trip to Punta Lobos in the afternoon is a fun excursion, but it was the one place I was cautioned not to go alone. I never did find out why it was off-limits to a single woman; however, I heeded the warnings. So get a group together to watch the *pangas* speed up onto the beach. You may even receive a fresh-caught fish from a smiling Pescaderan.

# # #

Just to the left of the highway north of Pescadero was one of my favorite places in the area. The Organic Produce Farm. This operation specialized in strawberries, most of which were shipped to California. There was a small outlet at the farm and you could buy all kinds of fresh picked fruits and vegetables — broccoli, cucumbers, lettuce, tomatoes, mangos, papayas, and more. The strawberries were ambrosia and the season extended from December through May. I had forgotten how heavenly the taste of produce picked ripe from the vine could be. I stopped often at the organic farm and loaded up on all those goodies. Besides being a blessing to those of us in the area, the farm employed about 200 people and was an asset to the economy,

# # #

San Pedrito was a fancy RV park north of Pescadero that had all the necessary amenities for the "pig rigs." The facilities were open to the public. I would drive over to do laundry and take a hot shower. The sardine effect was very much in evidence.

In Todos Santos, El Molino was an excellent park with a great restaurant. Both were nice to visit, but I did not wish to stay. I preferred my beach.

# # #

El and I played musical chairs with our rigs in that big campground. She had been out on a point of land and decided to move inside under some trees. She took the Airstream up by the back fence. I moved onto the point. El had some trouble with Saturday night revelers parked on the road outside the fence. She mentioned the incident to Francisco and he started locking the gate in the evening when he left. We then referred to our sacred beach as "the Nunnery."

# # #

I loved it up on the point. My only regret was looking down at *caballo* lying there by the firepit. Francisco and I were having coffee one morning and I haltingly told him I'd love to bring *caballo* to the new site. He could see the horse, too. Francisco and I hauled that heavy ironwood up to the point. Then, Francisco said, *"un momento"* and went over to the barracks. He returned with a digging tool and dug four deep holes. Francisco picked *caballo* up and put his legs into the holes. *Caballo* was resurrected! He stood guard over us on the knoll.

# # #

Sunday morning, day 28 of my now-scrubbed thirty day tour of the Peninsula, El and I were sitting at my table sipping coffee and gazing at the Pacific. I mentioned my need to get insurance coverage on Tessie. El said she was sure I could obtain a policy at the Vagabundo RV park in Cabo. She offered to go with me and suggested we drive down on Monday in case we hit a snag.

We loaded Ink and Gilly in the back of Tessie and got away from Cerritos early. Learned at Vagabundos that they were no longer writing insurance there — only in La Paz. I had my booklet from the border insurance. It listed an adjustor in San Jose del Cabo, so away we went on up the coast.

After a lot of walking and asking, we found a shopkeeper who gave us directions to the adjustor's house. When we got there, we found he had died two years before. So much for insurance.

# # #

San Jose is a delightful town — not as touristy as Cabo. Since we were there, we did some browsing and decided to have lunch. The dogs were getting hot in Tessie, so we put them on leads and walked across the street to a restaurant. At first, they weren't going to allow the dogs in, but we used our best powers of persuasion. The waiter eyed that elegant white poodle and my bouncy black Ink with some apprehension as he seated us in the patio. Gilly was always well-mannered. Ink seemed to realize that she had to be on best behavior, too. Both dogs settled on the cool concrete floor and were good as gold. El and I had a delicious meal in a lovely setting there in the patio by the fountain.

The Beach

By the time we got back to Tessie, she was shaded and cool. So, we put the dogs up and went into a posh boutique. We had a ball looking at and trying on beautiful Mexican clothes. El bought a spiffy white tunic and matching slacks. I purchased two sleeveless tunics, two overblouses to match, and a pair of white slacks.

Returned to Cabo San Lucas where we gassed up Tess. Just after we turned onto Route 19, El asked if I had ever been to the *Panadería* (bakery) in Cabo. We found a parking spot and visited what I found to be the best bakery in the Cape region. It was a typical *panadería*. You picked up a large tray and some tongs then proceeded to load the tray with all kinds of goodies. The *bolillos* and bread were in big tin lined bins, the sweet rolls and cookies were displayed on shelves. It was sumptuous. Then back to Cerritos — with no insurance, but some great clothes and an assortment of baked goods.

# # #

Tuesday, I knew I must go to La Paz for another try at insurance. El kindly offered to keep Ink. I got away by 9:30 a.m. since my existing policy expired at 1 p.m. I had hoped to find Vagabundo RV, but got lost in La Paz again. In driving around, I spotted a sign for insurance and went in. This place was an auto supply store with the insurance agent in an office in the back. He did not speak English, but understood from my old policy that I needed insurance. The cost here for one month was $116. I gulped and said write it up. Felt I had no choice. The agent did not take Visa so I left a deposit and dashed for the bank. Waded through the usual lines. Got back to the insurer at 12:40 and left with a valid policy in hand — good until April 15. I had twenty minutes to spare.

Needed to relax before driving home, so walked and browsed along the *malecón* for an hour or more. Had an ice cream cone — *helado* — and found it was good as Italian ice cream — *gelata*. Sat on a bench and enjoyed the breeze from the Gulf. Knew there had to be a better way to handle insurance. Knew, also, I did not want to be without it.

Left for Cerritos around 3 p.m. and got lost again. Drove in a circle — right past the Vagabundo RV park I had wanted to find. Tried again and was still wrong. The third time was a charm. I wandered onto Route 19 feeling like I had been dealing with Moncton, New Brunswick. Got to Cerritos about five, totally dragged out. After a few slurpy kisses from Ink and a short walk on the beach, I was fine. Thanked my gods and guides that we were insured and would not have to do that again. Little did I know.

# # #

Weekdays were slow and easy. Not so the week-ends when the local people flocked to the beach to play, fish, sing, and drink. One Saturday morning, the dogs and I were walking as usual. We'd wandered far down the beach, strolling along the Pacific, when a lad who had followed me finally approached. He propositioned me in Spanish. Even with my small command of the language at that time, I understood exactly what he had in mind. As he made his suggestions, he pulled aside his brief trunks and showed me his equipment. That really surprised me. I had fielded many propositions in my long lifetime, but never before had I been shown the wares. I didn't feel threatened at all, just surprised. I declined the offer and he accepted. He then walked along with us and we had a nice visit. One thing about the Mexican lads, unlike most American men, they take no for an answer and accept your refusal graciously.

When I got back to the campground, I immediately told El about the experience. I was still a bit shaken by it all.

El thought it was hilarious and soothed me. Together, we put it into perspective and had a good laugh.

This scenario became a week-end occurrence and I got rather used to the whole thing. El would sit in her Airstream and watch me and the dogs head out. Always some lad would stroll along behind us. When I'd get back to Tessie, she'd saunter down, grinning like a Cheshire cat and ask, "Well, how was that prick?" I'd shrug and say, "If you've seen one, you've seen them all." I had to assume this was a cultural thing — no proposition without showing the equipment.

After four episodes, the dogs and I refused to walk alone on week-end mornings. I waited for El and we would stroll together without any interference. We would break into gales of laughter playing out different scenarios: What if I just pointed at this lad's genitals and started to laugh? What if I told him I preferred women? What if I headed for him as if I was going to grab him? It was a strange experience, but it provided a lot of laughs for El and me. I never felt endangered by these handsome Mexicans, just amused that they felt the need to show what they were offering. I did wonder if this was usual procedure whenever they made any woman a proposition or if this was a special service for gringas only.

# # #

Toward the middle of March, El and I were having an early morning walk down the beach when she let out a whoop of surprise. There were turtle tracks! I didn't recognize them, but El did. This had to have been one huge *tortuga* from the depth of the tracks she made. They looked like the treads of a big tractor and we could re-create her visit. She had come in during the night on high tide. The tracks leading up the beach were much deeper than the ones going back to the sea. There were mounds of sand piled up where she had dug her nest. She laid her eggs, covered them with sand, then floated away to let nature hatch the babies.

Turtle eggs and the turtles, too, are a delicacy and there's a great problem with poaching. In spite of green sea turtles being protected, they're a gourmet meal. The people dig up all the eggs and eat them. Occasionally, a small Federal plane flies low over the beaches, but that's the extent of non-poaching enforcement in the Baja. The turtles are becoming an endangered species. El and I spent some time looking at the mounds of sand and I took pictures. We knew we'd have to hide this nest or the eggs would be gone.

On El's birthday, March 16, we took brooms, rakes, and shovels and obliterated all signs that mama turtle had visited us. Francisco helped with the subterfuge. He guessed the turtle weighed about 800 pounds. We marked the site with some rocks since we wanted to be able to watch the hatch and Mother Nature in action. We were pleased with our handiwork. Francisco, El and I sipped Martinelli's and toasted her birthday "celebration."

# # #

That Saturday night, I insisted on taking El into the restaurant at El Molino for a birthday dinner. We dressed in our Cabo finery and drove into Todos Santos. The weather was cool. We both needed sweaters, but the dinner was delicious. Roberto was at the bar and joined us. He was progressing with his training for the beauty salon. In talking, he mentioned that he was adept at carpentry. I suggested he come down to Cerritos with Adam and see if he could fix my door latch and the shelf in Tessie. He said he'd be glad to.

# # #

A few days later, Roberto and Adam arrived late

morning. Adam changed Tessie's oil, made a new latch for the hood, checked for rust spots, and gave Tess a general inspection. Roberto replaced the latch and secured the shelf in the closet. Suzie arrived and we all ate lunch together. What a blessing to have good help and up close and personal service from these two men.

# # #

At this time, El was planning to buy property in the Baja. Buy is a misnomer because land in the Baja is not for sale to foreigners. You execute a leasehold for 30 years, but you do not own the land. She asked me to join her on an expedition to look at property. I said I'd be glad to go along.

El was working with a Canadian girl who was married to a Mexican. Dale had lived in Todos Santos for 14 years and was knowledgeable. We all met at Bancomer. While looking at some old houses in town, Dale suggested that I should look at her *palapa* which was for rent. We all piled into El's pickup. Turned right and drove down the hill — past the Xerox copying shop — past the municipal pool which has never had water in it. Then along a eucalyptus-lined dirt road that was green and lush. The natives call the area *la huerta* (the orchard). It's where they have their gardens. Back up another hill over the bridge, a right at the second street and on up another steep, rut- and rock-strewn road to the top of the ridge. This was Barrio San Ignacio.

At the crest of the hill, Dale pointed out the driveway and we pulled in. There sat a small *palapa* — a round structure of dab and wattle construction with a high thatched roof — in the midst of lovely grounds. The Pacific was to the west and the Sierra de las Lagunas to the east. The village spread out below us, for this was one of the highest points in Todos Santos. The lot was narrow and deep. We got out of the truck and walked around a well-decorated patio to the one and only door.

The *palapa* was charming. Just one large round room with a step up to the sleeping area from the living and kitchen areas. What really grabbed me was the bathroom. There was a small, sunken tub! Just a small tub, but none-the-less a tub. After being in the camper for eight months and using communal showers, I would have rented that tub sitting under a palm tree. It was painted heavenly blue and it looked heavenly to me. The bathroom was well decorated with hanging plants and sea-shells and had a sky-light. It was alluring to say the least.

Dale insisted we walk the grounds. They were well-landscaped and inviting. Out back was a thatch-covered laundry area with an old GE wringer type washer, a storage shed with lots of books stacked on shelves. And to the front was a bougainvillea-covered gazebo with views of the sea, mountains, and the village.

The *palapa* had shuttered windows facing west. There were screens, but no glass — just wooden shutters that could be closed at night. The windows in the kitchen and bath were also screened, no glass. The kitchen had a small under counter refrigerator, a four burner stove, and a large sink, but no oven. The propane tank, which supplied gas for the stove and water heater sat outside next to the water heater. There was only hot water in the bathroom, but that was where the tub had to be filled. I found the *palapa* and grounds very appealing.

We tarried for a while. I could see that the chickens strutting around would give my Ink fits. I also was aware that there were no other gringos in Barrio San Ignacio. I told Dale I found the *palapa* charming, but made no commitments.

Drove back to the bank where Dale took her car. We followed her beyond Pescadero to a "Ranch" which was for

The Beach

sale (actually lease). There were 20 acres of land and the price at that time was $70,000. We spent the afternoon in that desolate spot. While El roamed around, I learned more about buying in the Baja. Everything is 30 year leasehold. The bank acts as fiduciary to hold leasehold papers for 1% of the appraised value which is usually about one-half the price. "Buying" entails half down with the offer and the balance when the *"fideo camiso"* is granted. There are no mortgages as we know them. On top of all this, there is a 30% transfer fee. I thought it quite an expensive undertaking for leasehold property.

El and I burned the midnight oil that evening. She was beginning to realize finding something she wished to buy and could afford was going to be difficult. We both agreed that the "ranch" was nothing she wanted. On the other hand, El was sure that I should rent Dale's *palapa*. Finally, making no earth-shattering decisions, we said our goodnights.

That night I had a vivid dream of the *palapa*. I was showing someone two track lighting rods that had been hung; one over the bed and the other over the serving bar in the kitchen area. I commented on how much I liked all the light. It was wonderful light and I was delighted. I woke from the dream feeling energized and happy. And, knowing I was to live in that *palapa* in Barrio San Ignacio.

At an earlier time in my life, I might have questioned the wisdom of living in a foreign land, I might have questioned what people would think. On this journey, I learned that I was well and truly led. The longer I traveled, the more I was certain that someone or something watched over me. The dream, so far as I was concerned, meant that I should stay. I accepted it and was comfortable with it.

After coffee, walked up and told El about the dream. She agreed that I should move to the *palapa*. So, my stay in

Mexico lengthened even more.

#

When Roberto was repairing Tessie, he mentioned that he felt some of the older teen-aged girls in Pescadero were fairly well trained in hair styling. They had set up a beauty shop: a different kind of salon. He urged me to come over for a hair cut. One morning, in order to boost the economy in Pescadero, I drove over to the shop. A group of beautiful, giggling, black-eyed young ladies welcomed me to the Salon. It was the patio of Bell's house — concrete floor, one small mirror on the wall in front of a barber chair with a small shelf of supplies. The patio was cool and enclosed with blooming bougainvillea. The sounds of birds singing and roosters crowing along with some traffic noise from the dirt road and, as always, children laughing, women calling to one another, and a distant guitar playing all added to the ambiance of this beauty shop.

The girls ushered me to the chair. Roberto asked me how I wanted what little hair I had styled. He, in turn, demonstrated to the girls with gestures which they understood. We all had a language barrier, but the girls were quick to learn and comprehend. Then, it was time for a shampoo. You haven't lived until you've had a cold water shampoo in a concrete sink on a bougainvillea covered patio in Pescadero with four "beauticians" hovering over you. The water was frigid! However, I survived and my teeth didn't chatter too much. All the girls took a turn at cutting with Roberto overseeing the process and admonishing, *"Suave, suave."* They did a nice job and got some needed practice. The cost of the cut and shampoo was $3.00. I left a *propina* for the gracious ladies and thanked them for their tender, loving attentions. Told Roberto I found his Beauty Shop the most unique salon I had ever visited.

#

I let the decision to settle in Todos Santos roll for a few days. Then, on the last day of March, I met with Dale and looked at the *palapa* again. It seemed even more inviting. We discussed terms and conditions. I would have taken a lease for a year; however, the rent would remain the same. I decided on month-to-month. That way, if living in the Barrio was impossible, I could bail out.

Dale asked $250 per month which included water, electricity, propane, and she picked up the trash. There was a tenant at the time, but he was to vacate in early April. Dale agreed to provide me with a desk, a floor lamp, and two more chairs in the gazebo. Ink had flopped tummy down with her legs behind her on the cool flagstone floor. She seemed to enjoy this thatched roofed hut we were going to call home for a while.

We drove down the hill to Dale's house and I wrote a deposit check for $250 and agreed to pay the last month's rent in advance when I moved in. As we were talking, I mentioned that insurance for Tessie was a major concern. Dale solved that problem immediately. She had forms for group insurance with Asimex, a company in Chula Vista, Ca. I could get insurance for a full year for $145. What an improvement over $120 per month with the Mexican insurers! I took that form gratefully. Dale seemed genuinely glad to have me as a tenant and I looked forward to living in Barrio San Ignacio. We both were pleased with our arrangement.

Since I was in Todos Santos, I had stopped at Bancomer for a cash advance before meeting Dale. The phones were not working. Since they had to call over to La Paz for approval and the current exchange rate to do a cash advance, it was impossible to get money with the phones out. The fellows suggested stopping back in about an hour.

Left Dale's and did just that, but the phones were still not working. So I had very little money that week-end. This is just one of the challenges of living in Mexico. You never know what's going to happen. A good sense of humor is a necessity. One day, I stopped for money and the fellows grinned sheepishly and informed me that the armored truck had not yet arrived. The bank had no money! I learned not to get too low before trying for a cash advance.

# # #

When Madrita came into heat, Ink learned more about the breeding habits of her species than she ever wanted to know. In spite of the isolation of the beach, two large black males arrived and had their way with Madrita. Female dogs are rarely spayed in Mexico and the dog population is out of hand. Madrita had obviously mated with these two males numerous times. This season was no exception. Ink was unsettled with all this mating and wanted to join the game, but the males had eyes only for Madrita. She was well serviced and there was no doubt that she would drop another litter of unwanted puppies.

Toward the end of the mating season, a young male arrived to check it out. He looked like he could be one of Madrita's offspring. The older males and Madrita tolerated the pup since he had no idea of what he was doing. In time, he decided Ink was more fun and that surely did bolster her ego. She couldn't understand why those handsome males didn't find her as attractive as Madrita. The two mating males never fought over courting rights. They had some sort of agreement worked out and each would take his turn with Madrita. They wasted no energy on fighting.

The puppy joined our dog compound and we named him Studly. After about a week, the black males were gone. Life settled into our usual routine of walks, swims, and

The Beach

chasing crabs.

# # #

Ink had become proficient at digging up the abundant crabs that lived under the sand. By this time, we had a retinue of dogs — Madrita, Studly, sometimes Gilly, and any other dog who had made its way to this place. Ink was designated crab digger. The others would stand by and wait until she had unearthed one. The crabs were quick and would scurry for the sea with all the dogs in fast pursuit. Occasionally, they would manage to grab one, but they didn't kill them, just played with them and then walked on. El commented that the beach looked like it had been shelled after one of our crab hunting forays. Ink loved all the dog company and was becoming bi-lingual. Whenever we met a new dog, she would ask, "Should I say hello or *hola*?"

# # #

The first of April, EL came down for coffee. It was cool and cloudy. This is the usual weather pattern for the southern tip of Baja. The Pacific waters are coldest during the latter part of February and into March and April. Most mornings are overcast and foggy along the beach. The Pacific was cold enough to keep Ink from her usual romps in and out. El and I did not swim either. She had come to tell me that a group of Marine Biologists were coming to Cerritos. They were interested in our turtle nest and planned to visit.

Around 4 p.m. three trucks filled with students and two professors arrived. One professor was from San Diego State and the other, Daniel, from the University of La Paz. The students in marine biology were from La Paz and Guadalajara. El and I led them down the beach to the covered site. Although they tried to locate some of the eggs, they couldn't find them.

No one was impressed with the size of our turtle. They told us that on the beaches of Michoacan the turtles weigh up to 1,000 pounds and they have 50 to 100 per night come to nest. This is where the bulk of research on green sea turtles is being done. The eggs are placed in hatching corrals to assure the turtles are safe. When the hatch comes, they help the tiny turtles get safely to the sea. That's not easy since all the predators are standing by to snatch up those tender morsels as they try to reach the water.

We gained a wealth of information from the professors and the students: Gestation is approximately 60 days — depending on the weather. Hatches usually occur around sunrise or sunset. They suggested we put some fine chicken wire around the nest, then take the little turtles closer to the sea in buckets of sand. This would cut down on predation and be easier than herding them. Daniel thought the hatch would occur anywhere from May 5 to 15. After 24 hours, we were to check the nest and dispose of any unhatched eggs as they contaminate the beach.

Cerritos was more northerly than most beaches where the sea turtles lay eggs. We were warned that they might not hatch. El and I assured the group that we were committed to seeing this hatch through and getting those little *tortugas* back to the sea.

It was a delightful session. Even though our nest was no big deal for the researchers, they were most generous with their time and information. The students were cold on the beach that day, but they all smiled and gave us help. We were impressed with the group. In Mexico it seems no one is in a hurry and it's refreshing. Bid them a fond farewell and thanks for all their help.

That evening, El and I ate together in Tessie. We were excited about the turtles and felt committed to seeing that

The Beach

those little fellows made it safely to the sea. El was concerned that I would be in Todos Santos, but I assured her I'd come to Cerritos for the hatch. We laughed and agreed that mother turtle had the right idea; just lay those eggs and swim away to let them hatch on their own. I thought the eggs would hatch on May 9. Since it was Mark's and Ink's birthdate, it seemed appropriate for the turtles, too. It had been a full day. We said our good-nights happy for the opportunity to see and possibly help Mother Nature in action.

# # #

That Sunday, a couple in a large diesel pick-up drove into the campground and inquired about parking up. Jack and Nadine had been parked on the public beach and the Saturday night revelries had gotten to them. I told them to come on over. That afternoon they pulled their trailer onto the ramp leading to the beach. They were a welcome addition. Jack and Nadine were from northern California, avid bird watchers, loved the Baja, and were great company. Nadine won my heart, when she was amazed that I would be 58 on April 4. I told her it was the good life I was leading.

I celebrated my 58th birthday there at Cerritos. It was a milestone. I never thought I would live to be 58. My mother had died at age 43. Both my father and brother died at 57. I always felt that I, too, would bow out at 57. But here I was on the most incredible beach in the world and I had made it. It had been a psychological barrier, but I was now 58 and felt I could go on for 50 more years.

Nadine took some photos of El and me. We had dressed and were going into Hotel California in Todos Santos for lunch. As we browsed and wandered around the village, I kept saying, "This will be my home town for a while." Truly, it had everything I wanted or needed. I was looking forward to living there even though I knew I would miss my nurturing beach.

As is the case in Mexico, all plans changed. Dale sent word that the tenant in the *palapa* would not vacate until May first. I then decided that I would not rent the *palapa* until May 15. That way I would be on the beach for the turtle hatch. Dale was amenable to that date as she wanted to do some repairs at the *palapa* before I moved in. So I had a reprieve. Settled in and savored my days at Cerritos even more, knowing they were coming to an end.

Some days, I would hit the beach running and singing at the top of my voice. Thank God, there were few people around. They would have been convinced this was a crazy woman with a herd of dogs who was totally amuck. I felt so alive, so in tune with this place, so joyful that I couldn't control all the gladness in me. I'd just run and sing and say thanks for being there.

Jack and Nadine stayed with us for 10 days. We all enjoyed our talks and walks together. When they left, they assured me they would visit me in my *palapa* in Todos Santos next year when they returned.

# # #

The Federales set up a road block on the highway just north of Pescadero. There were lots of armed soldiers standing on the highway. On my first stop there was also an English-speaking representative from the Tourism Department who apologized for the inconvenience. He explained that the United States was urging more road blocks such as this in Mexico to stop the drug trafficking. On that stop, the soldiers checked under the hood, looked in the glove compartment, and opened the back door of Tessie. I told the young Lieutenant who was in charge that I lived on the beach at Cerritos and went into Todos Santos often for mail and provisions. After that initial inspection,

The Beach

the fellows recognized me and waved me on through. They were there for two months. El and I invited the lads down to swim. It was hot, dusty, boring work for these young men, but they were always polite and friendly.

So far as I know, they never made a drug bust at that road block; however, they did capture an American who was staying at Los Pedritos. He had killed a man in California and was using the dead man's identification here in the Baja. I had talked to this man one day when I was doing laundry at Pedritos. He had three shair-peis with him and Ink was intrigued by those wrinkled dogs. We had a nice conversation. He didn't seem like a killer, but the Federales somehow nailed him. He was flown back to California and the shair-peis joined the soldiers at the roadblock.

# # #

El's daughter, the youngest of her six children, was coming for a visit of two weeks. Mary was to fly into the San Jose/Cabo San Lucas airport on the 26th of April. El left me in charge of the campground and Gilly. She drove to Cabo on the 25th to do some shopping. We both worried that Mary might be bored with strolling the beach and hanging out with us. Planned some touristy events. We knew Mary would enjoy the glass-bottomed boat ride around the harbor in Cabo. Planned a day in La Paz. There were dances in Pescadero each Saturday night. We hoped we could keep her entertained.

# # #

El and Mary arrived home about 4 p.m. on the 26th. As we all had tea and a small visit, I knew Mary would fit right in. She would love this beach as much as El and I did. Mentioned to them that the 27th marked two months of dry-camping at this incredible spot for me. Had anyone told me when I was in my forties that I would be happy living in an 18-foot camper, hauling water, taking cold water showers, and having only Mother Nature for entertainment, I would have said, "You're out of your mind." But here I was — perfectly content and happy with my world.

# # #

Roberto, Adam, and Suzie came out to the beach to meet Mary and make her welcome. She and Roberto hit it off well. El and I decided we did not have to worry about entertaining Mary; Roberto was happy to take over that department.

# # #

The traveling picture show came to Pescadero while Mary was with us. Since there are few movie houses in Baja Sur, the traveling show goes from town to town. It arrived in wagons that reminded me of old circus days in the States. A tent was set up with bleachers along the sides and benches down the middle. The stereo speakers were awesome and loud. Most of Pescadero turned out to see "Vengeance with a 30-06." The admission was less that one dollar American, smoking was allowed, and everyone from babes in arms to old men were at the movie show. In spite of an eardrum breaking sound track and benches so hard my butt ached, it was great fun. The plot wasn't hard to follow. A woman doctor was the heroine. Feminism had come to Mexico. Watching the teen-agers flirting on the bleachers was more entertaining. We learned that there would be another feature — a Mexican Western. El and Mary were unsettled by all the violence in "Vengeance". I couldn't sit another minute on those wooden benches, so we retreated to Cerritos. Still, joining the Pescaderons for the diversion of the picture show was some unplanned entertainment for Mary's visit.

Mary and El had to leave for Cabo for her return flight

The Beach

to the States on the 9th of May. Before they left, they arrived with a big box of cookies for Ink's birthday. The turtles had not hatched, but I assured El I would keep a close watch.

The dogs and I had the beach to ourselves. I sat that evening, watching the sunset with the dogs curled up at my feet. In reflecting on the past year, I granted it one of great adventure; a banner year in my life. I had been on my way to Italy this time in 1988. Now in 1989, here I was in Baja California. I couldn't decide whether I truly was becoming a gypsy or if it was the heady freedom of being able to follow my heart. And, I was more inclined to follow that inner voice the longer I traveled. Although my mind said, you must be crazy to want to live in the barrio, my heart said, this is where you need to be. Not at all logical. But what is logic? I found the intuitive side more tuned to my needs than the logical side. The more I listened, the better I was led. I sent happy birthday wishes and love to Mark, gave Madrita and Studly a pat, then Ink and I curled up in Tessie and fell asleep with the Pacific rolling steadily and surely.

# # #

Next day, when I returned from Todos Santos, El was home. We had a cup of tea. Both of us missed having Mary, but took comfort in knowing that she had a great time and thanked Roberto for his part. El mentioned that the Mother's Day Fiesta was that afternoon in Pescadero and we were invited. I suggested we go and lift our spirits. Then, too, we both left unspoken the fact that I would be moving into the *palapa* on the 15th.

We drove over for the Mother's Day festivities. The *ejido* had butchered and bar-b-qued an old bull — what symbolism. Every mother was entertained royally. There were two bands, the school children performed, and prizes were raffled off. All free for all mothers, but the men had to pay 10,000 pesos to attend. El and I joined the fun. We danced and ate and laughed. It was great to see all the women having such a good time and being waited upon — probably for the only day in the year. Got back to Cerritos just after dark in high spirits and grateful to the delightful people of Pescadero.

# # #

I had to start packing and putting my campsite in order. I had mixed emotions about moving from this beach; however, I wanted to live in that charming *palapa*. I worried about Madrita and Studly. I offered to bring food, and El assured me she would feed them. El was concerned about Madrita's pregnancy. I told her that old gal knew all about whelping, not to worry. I guessed that Madrita would drop her litter on the full moon in June. It was then that I made my commitment to the lovely, old female dog. I said, "You know, El, I think I'll have Madrita spayed. She's been at the mercy of her pheromones long enough. Another unwanted litter is ridiculous. When she's gotten these puppies weaned, I'll take her to our vet in La Paz and have her spayed."

Then, there were the turtle eggs. Nothing was happening. El and I decided that we should sit by the nest each evening and sing songs. El even moved her tent down and slept by the nest.

Those last few evenings by the turtle nest with a fire blazing were memorable. El and I knew I wouldn't be far away, but it wouldn't be the same. I knew I'd miss our enlightening talks and this sacred spot. We sat each night and serenaded the turtles, but to no avail. The little guys never hatched. What a disappointment. It had been very chilly and there was not enough heat to hatch them. The professors had warned us that this might happen. El and I took comfort in knowing that mama turtle could have cared less.

# # #

Francisco offered to wash some of the salt off Tessie before we went to Todos Santos. He took her up to the *pila* and did his usual fine work. I gave Francisco money for his labors which he, at first, declined. I insisted, knowing that Manuel was remiss in paying this beautiful man. Besides, Francisco had done so many nice things for me — fish he had caught, moving *caballo,* providing table and chairs, and just being such a good person. I insisted and he finally accepted my *propina* with a big smile. He could feed his family for a few more weeks.

# # #

Monday, the 15th of May, we pulled stakes at Cerritos. El left the beach before I did. She didn't want to say goodbye. Madrita and Stud chased us up the road for miles and it was wrenching. The tears were rolling down my cheeks as I drove the bouncy road for the last time. But, you must have endings before there can be new beginnings. We were on our way to yet another adventure. I had no idea what life in the barrio with the Mexican people would bring. Decided to welcome the opportunity and make no judgements until we tried it.

Life in Barrio San Ignacio

By the time we got to Todos Santos, I was composed. I had bonded strongly with Madrita and Studly. It broke my heart watching them desperately chasing us. Ink sensed my discomfort and nuzzled my arm as if to say she understood. I realized that I still had my best and most faithful companion with me.

We picked up some supplies. Stopped at the post office. There was a letter from Sam. That lifted my spirits even more. Then across the river and through the woods to Barrio San Ignacio.

Dale was at the *palapa* to greet us. She had taken the large bed out and put in a single, had replaced all the screens and planted extra flowers at the entry. There were linen cloths on both tables. I had one small round table in the living area and one for a work space on the sleeping level. Everything was spic and span and it looked lovely.

Dale gave me a key for the door. There was a surface mount dead bolt lock on the inside. As she was showing me how to use it, I noticed that the door was not flush and tended to swing shut. An old iron served as a door-stop. We went around to the laundry and she explained that the old washer was filled from the hose. In the storage shed was a big, oval galvanized tub for rinsing. There was a concrete pad with another sink for water, and a concrete washboard. There was a set of clothes lines in the yard. Quite a novel set-up. This looked rather challenging, but I was ready to give it a try.

She explained that the *pila,* which was above the shed was my water storage. The structure with the *pila* on top reminded me of a look-out tower. The laundry facilities were on the back with a thatch roof for shelter. No walls — an open air *lavandería.* The *pila* had been drained and recoated and was my water source for the *palapa.* All Todos Santos water was from deep artesian wells in the mountains. It ran through pipes by gravity flow into town. Then, there were some pumping stations that pumped the water into pyramid shaped storage tanks around town. The one for Barrio San Ignacio was up the hill from the *palapa.* The water from it also came by gravity flow and filled my *pila* which I used when I turned on a tap. There wasn't a lot of water pressure, but it was adequate. And, the water was sweet and delicious. It was so soft that I was always using too much soap. Really good water.

Dale visited for a while then was on her way. Ink and I made a lot of trips from the *palapa* to Tessie, slowly off-loading all our stuff. Found there was adequate storage space: a standing closet and drawers under the bed. It was fun exploring my new digs.

About dusk, Ink dashed for some chickens in the yard. I tore after her and the door swung shut — and locked. We were locked out of our house. I really felt like an alien in a foreign land about then. Knew there was no use going to the neighbors, since I couldn't speak enough Spanish to make myself understood. I could see the key to the door on the round table just inside the windows. Thought of driving down to Dale's, but wasn't sure I knew how to get there. It was a quandary and I felt so helpless. Finally, got my Swiss Army knife from Tessie and split the brand new screens Dale was so proud of. Split the one closest to the table along the very edge and managed to get my arm through and grab the key. I scraped my arm badly, but the worst hurt was splitting the new screens.

Didn't seem a propitious beginning; however, recouped standing up to cook dinner. What a treat it was to be on my feet while cooking. I had closed the pesky door, Ink was curled up on her feather pillow at the foot of the bed. Things were looking up. Went in and filled that heavenly blue tub and all was better. What a joy that hot, soothing soak was.

Got into bed and found I couldn't sleep with all that space around me. Tess had been a womb. Now there was an 18 foot ceiling and too much space. Then, too, the ocean was not rolling just outside my door. It was very still and quiet. I lay there thinking this too shall pass — I hope. Finally dozed off and slept fitfully that first night.

# # #

At 5:30 a.m. the roosters started to crow and the barrio came to life. I padded over and put on the kettle. Sat in bed listening to the noise — roosters in concert, lilting Spanish voices greeting the morning, dogs barking, and children chattering happily. It dawned on me as I sat there with my coffee that a thatched roof gave no protection from the sounds of the barrio. I could hear everything.

Ink had curled up next to me. She was adjusting to all the space better than I. Looked critically at my new house and decided that I'd need to make some adjustments. It was dark early in the morning — some sunshine peeking into the window in the kitchen and light from the skylight in the bathroom, but too dark. I wished I had the two track lights I had dreamt about. No matter, we could fix all of this. I knew I had to cut down all that space over my bed — just could not sleep well with that much space hovering over me. Decided some decorating was in order.

We didn't start early that first morning. I enjoyed standing to cook and wash my face. Ink seemed content to stretch out on the cool floor. I checked the door lock carefully before we went outside. The sunshine was warm. So, we filled the old GE with water from the hose and did some wash. Discovered there was no lid for the washer. In no time, I had an audience. Darling, black-eyed children came from everywhere and were enthralled with the churning paddle in the washer. I was happy for the company. Even tho' we couldn't talk much, we did exchange a lot of smiles.

Was resting and reading in the afternoon when Dale arrived. I was delighted to see her but I hated to tell her about the screen. By this time I had used some adhesive and glued it together. She probably never would have noticed, but I had to tell her. Dale said she'd get a few more keys made for me. I thought that an excellent idea. Being locked out was traumatic.   Dale had brought a copy of *Curso Intensivo,* the text she used to teach a small Spanish class. She asked me if I'd care to join. The class met from 10 a.m until noon on Tuesday and Thursday mornings. A group of *Norteamericanos* who now lived in Todos Santos attended and Dale thought it would be a class I would enjoy. I accepted immediately. Certainly needed to get over this language barrier with my neighbors.

# # #

Thursday morning I went to Spanish class. The group was friendly and helpful. They were already into book two of *Curso Intensivo,* but I thought I could study and catch up. It was great to speak some English with these anglo residents of Todos Santos. I had left Ink in the cool *palapa.* She did enjoy that. Curled up on her pillow and said she'd guard our new house.

After class, I stopped for some supplies. Found flea soap for Ink because she was bothered by the pesky fleas. At the Post Office, there was a Mother's Day card from Mark, saying "You're the bravest, nicest, wildest Mom a guy could have." Boy, I needed that!

# # #

The first two weeks were rough. I kept busy with Spanish classes, off-loading Tessie, doing wash, and walking each night with Ink. But I did feel the isolation. Always there was a sign that I should continue to give this barrio life a chance. One evening, Ink and I were doing our sunset walk when a car passed us then stopped. Two smiling ladies got out and exclaimed over what a beautiful dog Ink was. It truly lifted our spirits. It re-affirmed my knowledge that these were good, kind, lovely people; that I should take it slow and easy and see how it would go. I didn't want to change anything in the barrio, I just wanted to live and enjoy the life-style with these beautiful people. Too many Americans think that Mexico should be like Chicago. I loved the difference. If you take Mexico on her terms, life can be pleasant and satisfying. But, at times, in those first weeks, I had to retreat to the beach for a balancing walk and visit with El, Madrita, and Stud.

# # #

I had been having such fun settling into the *palapa*, I didn't think about Tessie's need for gasoline. Knew I had to get to Cabo soon. Loaded Ink and away we went. I realized the tank was low, but thought we could make it. Wrong! We had just started up the hill from a *vado* when Tess died. I knew immediately that she was out of gas. Couldn't make it up the hill, but did manage to get off the road. Luckily, there was a shoulder along this portion, but we were too close to the highway and on a curve. There we sat in the middle of nowhere without even an ocean view.

I wasn't happy. Could have kicked myself for calling the gas too close. It was the new city driving that

Life in Barrio San Ignacio

had thrown off my calculations. Forgot I wouldn't get such good mileage from Tessie in Todos Santos.

Patted Ink and told her we'd just have to wait for the Green Angels. This fleet of bright green pick-ups is the most comforting sight to stranded drivers that Mexico offers. The Green Angels patrol all the highways on a regular basis and are equipped to offer aid and help with minor repairs. They always carry gasoline and one of the Angels speaks some English. I was wondering just how soon one of the fleet might show up.

It was warm. We had water and a few cookies, so we stayed in the camper. There was no place to go. We were on a desolate stretch of roadway. Had just patted Ink again and told her we might have a long wait, when a car came up the hill and passed us. It slowed, stopped, then backed up. There were two young men and a girl in the front seat. I told them I had run our of gas. The two lads got out and asked if I had a hose so that we could siphon some gas from their tank. I had one in Tessie. They cut the hose and got to work siphoning fuel from their car. The young girl gave me a lecture on not letting my gas get low. She told me they were residents of Cabo. She was pleased when I told her I loved the Baja. The fellows got gas into Tessie's tank plus a bit in their mouths. They were sure I had enough fuel to get into Cabo. I offered to pay them and they refused, saying they were happy to help. Told me they would follow me into town. The girl ordered me to stop at the gas station at once and made me promise not to get low on gasoline again. We made it, and the kids waved as I pulled into the station. They were more delightful than the Green Angels. There are good samaritans the world over. Thank God.

# # #

Sunday, Adam, Suzie, Francisco and his family, and El

came for brunch and a house-warming. I had the toaster oven on the counter and four burners on the stove top. The joy of standing while cooking was very with me. Served meatballs and spaghetti, baked chicken in soy sauce, green salad, and flan with fresh strawberries for dessert. We all ate on the gazebo and everyone seemed to enjoy the feast. Suzie's daughter, Nellie, and her daughter, Beverly Anne, were with them now. They were a welcome addition to the party. All told me I looked very much at home in my *palapa*. Indeed, I was easing into the routine.

# # #

By this time the word had gotten out that the *gringa* was friendly and did not bite. Each afternoon I had a steady stream of kids stopping at the *palapa* on their way home from school. Mostly young girls about eight or nine. I would hear a tentative *hola* and would invite them in. One of the first phrases I learned was, *"No tengas miedo de mi perro — es muy amistosa."* The girls weren't sure about that big, black dog at the door, but soon learned that Ink was, indeed, friendly. She loved all of them and wagged all over in her greetings. They would exclaim, *"No tiene una cola. ¿Por qué?"* I had to say that I didn't know why Ink had no tail. She did have a little stump, but not the long, curling tails of most of the dogs in the Barrio.

These children were very curious about the *gringa* living among them. They were also quite sensitive. They'd start chatting away in Spanish, then stop, looking at me, and say, *"Ah, no entiende."* By this time I could say, *"Yo lo siento, no entiendo mucho, sin embargo, asisto clases en español."* The girls were so kind. They would sit at the counter and point out different objects and give me the names in Spanish. This was true with all the people. No one made fun of my fractured attempts to talk with them in their language. Everyone helped me. They were delighted

Life in Barrio San Ignacio

that I wanted to speak Spanish. At times, I would return to the *palapa* and wonder just what I had said as I was attempting to learn.

# # #

The weather was cool and foggy. Much more so than it should have been, I was told. I brought the quartz heater in from Tessie and plugged it in under my work table. It helped take the chill off my feet. Once the sun broke through, it warmed nicely. I continued to wash dirty clothes and get Tessie off-loaded. Had the clothes lines brimming one morning and the damned things broke.

Dale was a great landlady. Told her about my plight at Spanish class and she sent a man to put in new poles and re-string the lines. She was so much help and so kind. I had asked her if she minded if I move furniture and re-decorate a bit and she told me to have at it.

Moved the bed to the front wall and the work table over nearer the kitchen. Had found that the step up from kitchen and living area to the sleep/work area was very high. By the end of the day, I'd think twice before going up and down that step one more time. It was an even bigger step than the one into the camper. Knew my leg muscles were going to stay in shape.

# # #

I had time to explore my new home town. After Spanish class, I'd check out a few more *tiendas*. I was intrigued with the "hardware store". There was a variety of stuff in this shop, but what was so neat was that one could buy one nail, one screw, one sewing needle, one band-aid or one of most anything stocked in the store. I had great fun browsing that "hardware store." There were a number of clothing shops and grocery stores. Castros was on the main highway and catered to the tourists, Guillartes was the home town market. Then ISTE was a government-subsidized market. This was the place to buy paper products and cleaning supplies. Kept finding more and more goodies and feeling more and more at ease.

# # #

One day, after Spanish, I was going down the hill toward the *huerta*. Decided to stop and tour the Cultural Center. It was a large, one story concrete building and housed the library and some exhibits. The receptionist greeted me and told me to feel free to look around. There was no people availing themselves of culture that day. I gained insight on this lovely pueblo from the exhibits of the early history of Todos Santos:

The region had been inhabited by Indians long before the Spanish explorers arrived. They were hunter-gatherers with no permanent structures. Only their spectacular cave paintings remain as silent proof of life here. Baja is billed as the largest repository of cave paintings in the world. While the rock art of the Baja is similar to that found elsewhere, the half-red and half-black figures are rare and the use of yellow is very unusual. Most are high in the mountains and difficult to reach.

In 1535 Hernan Cortez sailed across from the mainland and attempted to found a colony at La Paz. It failed within a year. It was not until 1697 that the first lasting settlement in Baja California was founded in Loreto.

By the time an outpost mission was established in Todos Santos in 1723, the whole Pacific coast south of La Paz had been explored by the Spanish and found to be waterless with the exception of this oasis valley.

The full-fledged mission was established in 1733 and called *Mision Santa Rosa de Las Palmas*. The community was known as Santa Rosa de Todos Santos and eventually as Todos Santos (All Saints).

The original mission was completely destroyed in the

Cape-wide Indian revolt in 1734.

Soon after, a company of Spanish soldiers was dispatched from the mainland to capture and punish the offenders. The Todos Santos mission was rebuilt on a different site in 1735.

With the closure of the mission in La Paz in 1749 and the resettlement of the Indian converts to Todos Santos, the mission had its final name change to *Mision de Nuestra Señora del Pilar de Todos Santos*. The present day town fiesta is still celebrated on October 12, the day of the Virgin of Pilar.

The seeds of a secular economy were planted in 1767 when King Carlos III of Spain expelled the Jesuits not only from the Todos Santos mission but from the entire Spanish Empire. Then, the Franciscans, led by Father Junipero Serrá, took over the Baja missions They were not empowered to control all business and govern the indigenous people as the Jesuits had been. The process of granting land formerly owned by the southern missions to private individuals began.

In 1773, the mission was taken over by yet a third religious order, the Dominicans.

During Mexico's struggle for independence from Spain, economic aid was cut off to the Baja mission. It was during this time that people in Todos Santos began ranching and establishing homesteads in the area.

After Mexico's independence, lower California was opened for the first time to foreign commerce. Records indicate that a few ships had begun to put in at Todos Santos to buy meat, tallow, and hides from the ranchers.

The Mexican-American War of 1846-8, the expulsion in the 1860's of Emperor Maximilian, and the Revolution of 1910 barely touched the serenity of this isolated village.

In 1890, botanist T.S. Brandgee described Todos Santos

as a pretty place of 30 to 40 houses overlooking fields of sugar cane. Its prosperity during the last half of the 19th century and the first half of the 20th was based on sugar production. The handsome brick homes in the historic district and many of the public works were largely financed with sugar money.

In the 1950's, the water table began to dry up and production of *panocha,* the coarse brown sugar the area was famous for, ceased. Todos Santos suffered after the loss of its main crop and families were forced to move elsewhere. Although the water table gradually came back, water-intensive sugar cane cultivation was never reestablished.

The town's prosperity now comes from vegetable farming, orchards, fishing and ranching. The tourist trade has steadily grown since the completion of the Trans-Peninsular and tourism is seen as the industry of the future.

I left the Center praying that tourism would not overrun my lovely, tranquil village for a while.

# # #

Days were full of Spanish lessons, kids in the *palapa,* trips to the beach, checking the mail, reading and enjoying my new life. I was feeling more comfortable all the time. The kids helped a lot. A delightful group of children. All of them loved to look at the bathroom. No one near me had a bathroom or a bathtub and it was a novelty. With, *"¿Podemos mirar su baño?"* They would troop in and flush the toilet. It intrigued them. In spite of no bathrooms per se, the kids always looked like they had just been scrubbed. Wondered how their mothers managed it.

I was attempting to learn their names and it wasn't easy. Finally had the children write them for me. Then I really got proficient at saying *hola* to: Mirna, Zulema, Jorge, Lula, Dolores, Lupe, Juanito, Cariña, and Ramón. Most of the time the kids were fun, but occasionally they were totally hyper. I would chase them out and close the door for a little respite. Always, they would return and we'd start over.

I had the radio inside and often would play jazz tapes which the kids adored. They all loved to dance and we'd dance and sing and have drinks and cookies. The radio helped, too. During the day I could get a station from La Paz. The call letters are indelibly etched on my brain: *Radio Cutural de La Paz con mil watts de potencia.* In the morning there was a program patterned after Sesame Street, but in Spanish. Afternoons were a mix of classical and jazz music. That station helped greatly with my learning the language. At night, I could get some radio waves from the States, but faintly. Tended to stay with the Mexican stations and see how much I understood.

I studied Spanish a lot. After dark, the barrio was quiet and I had nothing else to do. Since the class was on Book Two, I had to review the first book and also try and keep up with them in Book Two. Felt I'd never learn all the verb forms, but kept working on it. Then, too, I had Little Brother plugged in and wrote long, lengthy letters to everyone. It kept my English up to date since I didn't use it much in conversations in Todos Santos.

# # #

The last Sunday of May, I packed lunch and Ink and I left the Barrio for some time on our beach. Ink was suffering from flea bites and needed a salt water swim. We stopped at the produce stand and bought a flat of strawberries, since the market would close the end of May. Got to the beach about 11:00 a.m. and found no dogs and no El. We parked and took a soul-lifting walk. Sat on our cliff and enjoyed the oneness with nature. When we got back to the campground. El was there. She had been in

Pescadero making phone calls. We lunched and talked. The water had warmed and she swam each day, but there were sting rays. Some surfers had suffered painful stings. Ink was not bothered while she romped in that soothing salt water. I told El that I was enjoying each day more and more in the Barrio, but it still was a big adjustment and I had to bide my time. Spent a quiet afternoon of good conversation with a dear friend. Madrita never appeared, nor did Stud, but Ink and Gilly had a good chat, too. Before I left, I picked some eucalyptus leaves. I found that steeping the leaves and then dousing Ink with the water helped rid her of the pesky fleas for a short time. Nothing worked very well on those *pulgas*. Got back to the *palapa* about five. The barrio was very quiet. Treated Ink, had a hot tub, and climbed into bed to read I Ching which El had lent me.

# # #

Monday, I made strawberry jam and played house. Did four lines of wash. Stood there in my outside *lavandería* and thought to myself, where else can you do your wash and get a suntan at the same time? The new poles and lines were great. And, the women in the neighborhood all greeted me as we were doing laundry in our backyards. Swept and dusted, did some Spanish and felt, for the first time, I was at home.

# # #

Should have known all couldn't continue so well. The last day of May, I decided to wash my sleeping bag in the old GE. No problem until I tried feeding it through the wringer. Not sure what happened. The bag wound around the wringer and it would not let go. I spent hours trying to get the sleeping bag unwound, but to no avail. I had to give up because my hands and arms were mangled. Left it all knowing I'd see Dale at Spanish class the next day. Had a hot tub and hopped into bed early — not only to escape the cool weather, but to ease my frustration.

# # #

Dale came up to the *palapa* after Spanish class. The two of us together could not make that old wringer let go of the sleeping bag. Dale, ever resourceful, suggested we take the whole mess to a small shop in Todos Santos. We threw the wringer, still holding onto the bag, into the back of Dale's pickup and headed for town. The Mexican fix-it-man shook his head and went to work. He had luck and in about an hour I was home with the wringer and a soggy sleeping bag. Hung the bag over the lines. Cursed the wringer and vowed I'd not let it near my sleeping bag again.

# # #

Next morning, we drove out to Los Pedritos and gave the bag a hot water wash. There was no one in the campground, so we had full use of all the facilities. Threw the bag into the dryer and Ink and I had a walk along the beach. The bag was none the worse for wear, thank God. I was sleeping in it since the weather continued cool. We were home by noon with a clean bag and a grudging respect for the wringer.

# # #

Spanish class was scheduled for Monday, June 5. I ran into El and her son, Gabriel, at the Post Office on my way. How serendipitous. Gabriel had arrived from Guadalajara and planned to spend some time at Cerritos. A tall, handsome lad and a welcome addition to our family. He hoped to attend the University at La Paz, but would be with us until fall.

# # #

Drove out to the beach on the 8th. Madrita was there to greet us along with El and Gabriel. Madrita was heavy with pups and I was sure she'd drop the litter at full-moon.

We all agreed it would have been better for mother turtle's eggs to hatch and Madrita to abort. Gabriel helped load *caballo* into El's truck and we brought my horse home to the *palapa*.

# # #

Saturday, it was brunch for El, Gabriel, Adam and Suzie. Gabriel brought Francisco's digging tool and he and Adam dug holes in the yard and planted caballo. He was resurrected once again and now stood guard over the *palapa*. I named him Picasso and was happy to have him grazing in the garden. Adam had bought a new fuel pump for Tessie and installed it. We all pigged out and enjoyed the sea breeze in the gazebo. Everyone was ready for warm weather.

# # #

Wednesday, the 14th, El and Gabriel picked me up at 8:30 and we were off for a day in La Paz. Gabriel needed to see about the University. El and I had shopping to do. It was such a pleasure not to drive. And, I knew El could get out of La Paz without circling round and round. My most cherished acquisition that day was netting for over the bed. El and I found some beige nylon in a small shop and I bought a long length. El told the clerks it was to be for my wedding gown and they presented me with a delicate ribbon bedecked silk flower arrangement. El showed me around some areas of La Paz I had not visited before: A seed shop with bins of rice, pasta, and beans, the health food store where we ate lunch, a book and record shop which had some great jazz and classical tapes. Even found batteries for my camera.

Shopping is very different from the States — no one-stop shopping centers — but rather many small *tiendas*. The personalized attention was well worth the effort of walking and looking and finding what you needed. Gabriel got information he needed at the University. We agreed it had been a productive day.

On the drive home, Gabriel asked how I was going to hang my netting and I told him of the bamboo stalks out back. Said I'd have to take some time, but was sure I could come up with something. He offered help in getting the netting hung when I was ready. We didn't get home until almost six. Ink was happy to see me, but told me she preferred staying and guarding the cool *palapa* rather then driving around in circles with me in La Paz.

# # #

I made it to Spanish class the next morning, but was weary. The class continued to be a good learning and social break. One of the gals mentioned that with the summer solstice on June 21, the sun would be directly overhead at noon and there would be no shadows. This because of Todos Santos' location on the Tropic of Cancer. Made a mental note and thought I'd have to check that out.

# # #

Sunday, Ink and I had lunch at the Hotel California. Manuel, the manager had kindly loaned me a quarter when we were on our way to Los Pedritos to wash the sleeping bag and I had to repay him. He and his wife were a lovely couple and Manuel spoke excellent English; however, he insisted that we speak in Spanish. The dining room was uncrowded and cool. Ink flopped on the floor and I had a quiet meal. Manuel told me he thought I was doing well with my language endeavors and I appreciated that.

We drove on out to Cerritos for a walk and talk with El and Gabriel. Madrita, still heavy with pups, waddled along with us on the beach. I had survived a month in the Barrio and was not ready to give up. El asked how it went. I could talk frankly with this dear friend. Said, at times, I felt like an alien and was really weary. El pointed out that

I had made two trips to La Paz, a trip to Cabo, had had two brunches, and had leaped feet first into four hours of Spanish a week. Her advice: slow down and smell the roses — after all, this was the land of mañana.

# # #

The kids loved Picasso. Most afternoons there would be four or five of them astride my trusty steed. I used hammer and nails and we tacked a dry palm frond on him for a tail. The kids were a daily occurrence. They would all stop on their way from school and tell me about the day while we sipped juice and ate cookies. I, most of the time, loved the company. It's always the children who are first to meet and greet a stranger. But, slowly, the adults were accepting this *gringa* in their midst, too.

I brought some of the bamboo stakes around to the portal and took a look at them. They would make a sturdy frame for over the bed. Measured the bed and cut the bamboo to fit. Found I could not nail it; it just splintered when I drove the nails in. Had some kite string in the camper and lashed the corners. That worked well.

Dale was intrigued with my decorating project and suggested that I wrap the bamboo with material and then just drape the netting over and it would stay. Found the leftover material from Tessie's new draperies and used it. Things were moving right along. The kids would sit on Picasso watching all this. They accepted the *gringa loca* and her chores.

# # #

The 21st, I told Ink to guard the *palapa* and left early for a run to Cabo San Lucas. Needed gasoline and wanted to find rugs for the *palapa*. Knew Ink would not enjoy the heat. Indeed, the gulf side of the peninsula was always 10 to 20 degrees warmer than Todos Santos. Got gasoline, then parked Tessie and shopped. Bought three Oaxaca cotton rugs — two with white backgrounds which I knew was impractical, but loved the lightness it would bring to the dark *palapa*. These were for the sleeping level. The third was an abstract design echoing Picasso. It was so handsome that I knew it should go in the living room. Stopped for an iced tea at a sidewalk cafe, then the *panadería* and headed north. Something perked me and I glanced at my watch. It was noon. I pulled off the highway and got out. And, I had no shadow on this solstice day. It was eerie. There was a herd of goats by the roadside and they had no shadows either.

Stopped at Cerritos with some *panadería* goodies for El and Gabriel. Madrita had dropped her litter on the full of the moon. She had a nest under a large bush close to the point where I had been parked. Gabriel had checked and there were eight pups. Not what the dog population needed. Madrita heard me and came to tell me of the birth. She was fine and so was the unwanted litter. My desire to have this old gal spayed strengthened.

I left a bag of food for the new mother. El and Gabriel made an appointment to come in Friday and hang the netting. I got home and finished wrapping the bamboo. Wondered how we were going to mount the frame to the beams since I had been unable to find anything suitable. That evening on our walk, I spied four pieces of wire hanging over a fence. Just ask and you shall receive. We were back on *ejido* land and there was no sign of anyone, so I said a silent thank you and took the wire home.

# # #

Woke at 5:30 a.m. with the decorating project on my mind. Stripped the bedding, the table clothes, and sundry items for washing. El and Gabriel got to the *palapa* about eleven. Gabriel took over. He had those found wires in place in no time. We tried the netting and he pointed out that if we cut the material and tied it over the top, there was enough to hang down the sides to the bottom of the bed. Gabriel secured the top netting, cut the yardage and then tied those ends to the frame. *Voila!* We had the bed totally enclosed and didn't have to sew anything. The finishing touch was the flower bouquet the clerks had given me. Gabriel pinned it to the top corner of the bed. While we were having lunch, El and Gabriel both teased that they were sure I was not living alone in what was beginning to look like a bridal suite. I finished up with the rearranging by 4:30 then stood back and looked at the handiwork. The *palapa* was light and airy and, to me, just lovely.

Ink and I walked and had dinner. I took a hot tub, climbed into a clean bed and surveyed the *palapa*. I felt like Cleopatra sitting in her barge floating down the Nile. Everything was clean and sparkling. Granted a bit more foo-foo than my usual quarters, but it was pleasing. Slept that night soundly and well. The snugness of that netting made me feel better; more like I was in Tessie's womb.

#

Dale came by Saturday morning and we had coffee. She approved of the decorating. Asked me if I'd like to have a phone. At first, I said, "no-way." We discussed the phone rates in Mexico and the difficulty in getting through to the States. Dale pointed out that it was much cheaper for the kids to call me than for me to call them. Mexico has very high phone rates — not within the country — but for long-distance calls the tax was about 52%. Dale and I discussed phones some more and I decided it was a good idea. She said she'd order one and have her men come up and dig a trench for the line. She cautioned that the phone might be installed within two weeks or two months. Asked me to try and compute the tax assessed on the bill. In 14 years, she had never been able to work it out. So, my foo-foo *palapa*

Life in Barrio San Ignacio

was going to be wired for a phone. I really was settling in. Had some misgivings about a phone imposing on my privacy; however, liked the thought that my sons could reach me if they needed me.

# # #

I had promised El and Gabriel that I would go to Cerritos on Sunday and feed Madrita. They were going over to the Gulf side for the week-end. Ink and I got there late morning. The little mother was waiting and hungry. Gabriel had made a cozy shelter for the puppies under one of the barracks buildings. He had enclosed a run for them and they seemed to be thriving and happy. Madrita could hop the barricade and escape those voracious little devils. She needed some rest from eight, hungry pups. Francisco was at the park; very hung-over. He told me there had been a great party in Pescadero Saturday and he had had *"tan más cervezas."* He informed me that there were five males and three females in this litter. No problem giving the males away; the females would be another matter. Ink and I took a short walk, had lunch, and left early. Francisco wanted to lock up and go home to nurse his headache. Madrita and the pups were fine and ready for a siesta after a hearty meal.

I stopped at Pilar's and tried reaching kids. No go Scot and Juli, but did get through to Mark and Lois. Best news was that they were planning to come to Todos Santos for Thanksgiving. Told them I'd be getting a phone and that Madrita had her puppies. It was always great to talk with the kids. What a nice visit to look forward to. Seemed I was to stay in the Barrio so that my kids could come and visit this different culture.

# # #

With the end of June, the weather was becoming warm and balmy. Friday night there was a *baile* at El Molino.

The sounds of *salsa* throbbed all over Todos Santos. When there's a dance, the whole town vibrates. The Mexicans love their music loud. Ink and I sat on the portal and enjoyed the concert until 2 a.m.

Next morning, I had sipped two cups of coffee sitting under the netting before it dawned on me that Ink was not up. I had another cup and still no good morning greeting from my Ink. When I patted her, she seemed reluctant to move. Lifted her head and her muzzle was horribly swollen. I checked, but could find no stinger. Put some ice cubes on her nose. She was really under the weather and stayed curled on her pillow all day. I suspected a scorpion. She was fighting some venom in her system for sure. It was the first time in her life that she would not wag her tail nor eat. She looked pathetic and yet funny with her swollen snozzola. Slept most of the day. In the evening, she drank a little milk and took some canned food. Next day, she was much better, but not quite her jubilant self. Thought perhaps Ink would have to move onto the bed under the netting. Scorpions loved to hang out in the thatched roof. One must have dropped to the floor and bit my Ink while she was sleeping.

# # #

The tropics was an excellent arena for creepy-crawlies and critters of all kinds. They were free to wander in and out whenever they chose since the roof did not deter them. Also, the door did not fit well. The frogs would come under it each night and jump into Ink's water bowl in the bathroom. They were striking frogs — bright orange and lime green. At times they would hop into the sunken tub and were unable to get out. My morning chore was to climb into the tub and gather the frogs. I'd put them outside, but each night they returned. They were among the most welcomed of the visitors.

Life in Barrio San Ignacio

Cockroaches were everywhere, along with mice, moths the size of hummingbirds, and lots of ants and mosquitos. Since bugs didn't bother me, I learned to live in peace and harmony with them. Except for the mice. Finally had to place some traps around since they were dancing across the partition between the bath and main room each night. There were no cats in the barrio, hence the huge mouse population. When they started getting into the drawers under the bed and gnawing on my clothes, they had to go. I baited the traps with peanut butter or avocados, no cheese. Was catching two or three each night and throwing them into the garbage cans until Dale told me to flush them down the toilet as they were good for the septic system.

The rest of the critters, I tolerated and observed. There were moths that would flit into the *palapa* at night attracted by the light. I could not bring myself to kill them since they were as large as hummingbirds and quite vividly colored. I spent hours herding them out the door. Bought little coils that could be lighted and would give off protecting smoke for the mosquitos. As for the *pulgas* (fleas), Ink and I never found a solution. I took to hand-picking them from my poor bitten dog. A salt water swim or flea soap or eucalyptus dip would give Ink relief for a few hours, but the *pulgas* were always with her. She, too, accepted it as the way of life in the tropics.

Besides the creepy-crawlies we had lots of domestic animals in the Barrio; goats, pigs, horses, cows, and heaps of chickens. One morning, Ink and I opened the door and there were two pigs standing in the yard. They belonged to Ramon, the young lad who lived behind us. He kept them tethered, but they loved to slip away and explore the neighborhood. I began calling them Tweedle-dee and Tweedle-dum. They provided excitement from time to time running through yards with Ramon in hot pursuit.

The chickens were Ink's greatest irritation. We had a fence of sorts, but they wandered in and out of the yard. Ink knew they had no business being in her territory. She would pounce on them when she could. Although she never bit one, the poor Mexican chickens died of fright when that big, black dog pounced. It was not the proper way to meet my neighbors — walking around the barrio carrying dead chickens — inquiring who owned them. I gladly reimbursed them for their loss.

After three dead chickens, I tied Ink to a post on the portal with her long lead. Could not have my dog eating the neighbors' food supply. The timing was propitious. Some older kids arrived one morning with a dead rooster claiming that Ink had killed him. By this time, I was able to understand and countered with, *"Lo dudo."* I walked them around the patio and showed them that Ink was tied. Thanks to my Spanish classes, I was able to pull up, *"Mira. Mi perro no puede matar su pollo."* They left with heads hung. I realized I had saved myself from paying for every dead chicken found anywhere in the Barrio. And, I kept Ink on a long lead from then on. She didn't mind and could wander in and out, but could not pounce on the chickens.

# # #

Sunday, Ink had recovered and I left her to attend a goat roast with Dale. We arrived at the fiesta about 3 p.m. There was a nice mix of Mexicans and Americans. Antonio and Ruth, the hosts were Mexican and American respectively. The goat was buried in hot coals and simmered in a pit all day in sauce. It was really delicious. There was dancing and singing and guitar playing. Great food and great festivities. I met two interesting women from Cabo San Lucas: Anita, a striking, blond who spoke Spanish fluently. She and her husband had owned an art

Life in Barrio San Ignacio

gallery in Cabo, but returned to the States when he became ill. After his death, Anita, chose to live in Cabo and opened another gallery. Maurine was a younger woman, probably in her 40's and originally from Canada. She had just worked her way from Alaska to Cabo and had a great sense of humor. An international group of people, enjoying themselves and the tasty goat bar-b-que.

# # #

The fourth of July is our Independence Day. It's a non-event in Mexico. No celebration: business as usual. We had Spanish class, so I did my usual rounds: Post Office, bank, mercado. Took Ink with me and we drove out to Cerritos to see El. I chided her for not flying the flag. A group of gringos were having a celebration at Los Pedritos, but I opted for a visit with El and a quiet walk on the beach. Ink wanted to tell the dogs about her swollen snozzola and her nasty bite. She was back to her exuberant self and even played with the puppies for a bit. Madrita's litter was growing and prospering. Those pups were far advanced at three weeks compared to litters I had raised. Guess they mature quicker in the tropics. Gabriel was giving them food in a bowl and they could handle it well. This, of course, delighted Madrita. They were able to run after her and were driving her a little frantic with their demands for milk. Of the eight, there were seven who favored the two black studs who fathered them, but one female was a dappled white who looked just like Stud. Some recessive gene in the background, no doubt. And, it did make us think that Stud was one of Madrita's sons.

Got home about 5:30 and scrubbed Ink. She ate a big dinner, we walked, and she slept well being rid of voracious fleas for a short while. *Pulgas* were part of life in Todos Santos and Ink tolerated them fairly well. Guess it bothered me to see my gal sitting and scratching just like all the Mexican dogs

#

On our evening walks, a young pup would run out to greet us when we strolled one road on the *ejido* land. Ink thought he was great fun and they would romp and play together. One evening, a man walked up the lane, saying that the pup was his. Mario looked like an Inca. I could understand him very well and we started sitting on a rock by the roadside and talking. He had worked in the farm fields of California, but was now retired and back in his home town. He had a small concrete house and an acre of *ejido* land with glorious views of the ocean, village, and most of Barrio San Ignacio. He told me I spoke Spanish very well and he'd be happy to tutor me. I was noncommittal, but asked my Spanish class what they thought. I did not want to go against cultural norms and was not sure it was proper to visit his house. Everyone encouraged me to take advantage of the lessons.

One afternoon, Ink and I wandered over to Mario's for some tutoring. The dogs played and Mario, who quite obviously had given some thought to the lessons, started with having me go through the alphabet. He had a newspaper and helped me with reading and comprehension. We sat on chairs outside the house looking at the ocean and speaking Spanish. Mario was helpful and intelligent. I never met anyone in Todos Santos who could not read and write.

We met once a week for a while and Mario gave me a Spanish version of Hermann Hesse's *Steppenwolf.* I was amazed and asked him if he had read it. He told me, yes, three times. I was impressed since I had never been able to wade through that novel in English.

#

Mario would stop at the *palapa* for tea and conversation.

Life in Barrio San Ignacio

I enjoyed his company and Ink thought Sultan, his dog, was a good buddy. All was going well until one evening when my next door neighbor arrived with her youngest daughter. Elisa was agitated, I could tell. I had trouble understanding her, but her daughter, Hermalinda, was one I could comprehend. We all had a cigarette and some tea. Then, with Hermalinda's help, Elisa warned me that Mario was a *borracho* and never to allow him in the *palapa* after dark. He was her brother and she didn't want him taking advantage of me. If I understood correctly, he had tried to molest all four of her daughters. I promised her I'd be careful.

Mario had been nothing but kind and helpful to me. Now his own sister was saying he was a drunkard and not to be trusted. I had a feeling that there was more here than I would ever understand. I did not go to his house any longer, but Mario would stop and visit. I did not want to offend my neighbors, but didn't want to hurt this man who had been so kind.

Elisa and her family took me under their wings. She and Jorge had four daughters: Mercedes who was married and lived in Ensenada, Carmela who lived in La Paz with her husband and young son, Mirta also married and living in Todos Santos with two children who were fixtures at the *palapa,* and Hermalinda, still single and living at home.

Jorge, the patriarch of the family was a buddha of a man. When he spoke all the women came to attention. He scared me to death, when I first moved in. He didn't seem to appreciate a *gringa* living next door. Whereas Elisa and the girls were curious and friendly, Jorge ignored me completely. All that changed in time. I treasured the friendship of the family so did not encourage Mario to visit. I knew it unsettled Elisa.

# # #

July was warm and lugubrious. Dale brought me an oscillating fan. With the sea breeze and no windows, the *palapa* stayed fairly cool. I loved the warmer weather, but Ink would sprawl on the floor and catch the breeze from the fan each afternoon when we took our siesta. All business stopped from one until four in Todos Santos. I embraced this very civilized custom wholeheartedly. When the roosters wake you at 5:30 in the morning, you're ready for some quiet time after lunch. A few of the food markets stayed open; however, the banks closed for the day at 1 p.m. Most small shops closed and even the post office closed for siesta then re-opened at four. Seemed the way to live.

# # #

One evening about 4:30, Ink and I made a trip to the post office. On the way home, we decided to do some exploring. Instead of taking our road up the hill, we drove on out the main road. Passed the elementary school which was a colorful one story building. The playground was well equipped. The building and grounds looked well kept and inviting. Turned off the dirt road and headed across some fields looking for a place to park and walk another beach. Managed that, but the drop-off to the ocean was steep. Ink didn't even venture down that steep incline for a swim, but we had a lovely walk. In trying to retrace our tracks, we got hopelessly lost. Kept bouncing around fields and coming to dead ends. Luckily, met two men who helped me get turned around and advised me to follow the electric lines and I would find my way. It was another small adventure we hadn't anticipated.

# # #

The telephone was installed in two weeks. I named Dale the miracle worker. Now I was in touch with the world, but had mixed emotions about that phone. Knew it was

The south cove,
Cerritos Beach

Madrita, Studly,
Ink and friend.

Sunset at Cerritos

Hermalinda, Mirta, Lula and Jorgito with Ink at North Beach near Todos Santos

My laundry facilities at the palapa

Interior of my palapa

Life in Barrio San Ignacio

good that my sons could reach me if they needed me. I also found myself wasting a lot of time wondering if and when they might call. Decided sitting and waiting for the phone to ring was futile. Told myself if anyone wanted to talk and didn't reach me, they would call back. In a small way, the phone was a comforting imposition.

# # #

Spanish classes were canceled until August 15 since most of the students were going to the States. I kept practicing and studying and talking. In one of our conversations, Mario made an astute observation. He was telling me how much my neighbors appreciated that I wanted to speak Spanish. He said, "most Americans learn to say, *'una cerveza más, por favor,'* and that's the extent of their desire to speak the native language."

With no classes, I had time for more letter writing. An excerpt from one sent to my Aunt Dora sums up my feelings:

"I think so often of the memories you've shared with me of your childhood because this village seems to be what our country was early in this century. It's still an agrarian community with an easy pace where people have time to visit, the kids roam around and play games, everyone knows her neighbors, there's no crime, and life is easy. Not much like the frantic pace in the States where everyone is in a hurry. By our standards, I'd have to say the people are very poor. They don't have many material things; however, they are more joyful and content than most people I know. There's always the sound of laughter, singing, music playing, and children's voices. Also, the roosters crow, the cows moo, dogs bark, goats bleat, pigs snort. I'm sometimes inundated with sound — not traffic noise, not airplanes, just people and livestock. I can tell from your letters that you worry about my safety here in a foreign land. Rest easy, my dear Aunt. I'm safer here than I would be anywhere in our own country, believe me."

# # #

The 26th of July, it rained — the first rainfall in eight months. Ink and I took our evening walk in a gentle shower. It rained again on the 27th — enough rain to make me cancel a trip to Cabo. Felt the *vados* would be running full and I'd have lots of delays, so stayed home and enjoyed a cloudy, rainy day. The thatched roof had two small leaks; and, with the rainfall, the scorpions kept dropping out of the thatch. I lay that night under the netting, counting bugs that couldn't fall into my bed. Ink slept with me. away from scorpions on the floor.

# # #

A young couple from Texas, newly arrived, gave a big bash Friday evening at the Loca Langosta. They kindly invited me. Decided I should become acquainted with the expatriates in the village, so accepted.

The party was scheduled for 7 p.m. I arrived at 7:30 and was early. About 8 festivities got under way. There was a great Mexican band, lots of dancing, lots of drinking, and lots of sweating. It was a hot, humid night.

The guests were a varied and interesting group. I met Julian and Enzio, both artists who lived up the street from me. Julian was a native, Enzio was from Italy. A number of young men from the States were in Real Estate in Todos Santos and Cabo. Spoke with a gal visiting from Austria who planned to move to Todos Santos. The daughter of the ex-governor of Baja Sur and her mother, who had been a movie star in the U.S. were there. Had a long talk with a Mexican psychologist from La Paz who was thinking of moving his practice to Todos Santos. Sat down next to a delightful woman from Washington state visiting her kids and thinking of moving here. Lynn and I had a great talk.

She had divorced after 26 years. Felt life in Todos Santos might be fun. I told her I thought so. Juan, the Spaniard, and my favorite dancing partner was there. It was a varied, homogeneous group

Dinner wasn't served until 9:30. The entree was baked rabbit, baked potato, refried beans, and potato salad. Quite tasty. I don't drink so was aware of the quality. Most everyone, by this time, was feeling no pain. The drinks were free and downed rapidly. It was hot and humid, no breeze at all and everyone was sweating profusely. I had a good time. It was a chance to meet many people I would never have seen in Barrio San Ignacio.

At 10:30 I opted for my *palapa* even though the cake had not been served. Said my good-night to the hosts, to Lynn, and some other guests and went home. I had thought the Barrio was noisy, but this warm evening it seemed blissfully quiet. Ink and I strolled round the garden, then called it a night.

# # #

The last Sunday of July, the kids called through. Said they had no trouble with the direct dialing. 'Twas good to talk with both Mark and Lois. I was especially glad to discuss what to do about my car which had been stored in Berchie's garage in Las Cruces. She had written saying she needed the space. I could see nothing to do but fly to the States and take care of my obligation. Berch kindly agreed that September would be soon enough; however, I had to start thinking about that task. No matter how long you live, there's always something to handle. I didn't want to make the trip, but could see no other way.

Letters were shuttling back and forth. It warmed my heart that everyone was looking forward to my visit. El had offered to keep Ink at the beach. In my heart of hearts, I knew I wanted to stay in Barrio San Ignacio, not fly to the

United States.

#

Ink and I had a small celebration on the first of August. It was my older son, Scot's, birthday and we had now been one full year on the road. Never did I think when we left Las Cruces we would travel so far and so long. However, here we were happy in our thatched roofed *palapa* in the barrio and looking forward to more adventures. Ink and I still enjoyed each other's company. Wondered if two people who had been together in an eighteen foot camper traveling for a year would feel that way.

#

The rains continued and the two small holes in the roof kept leaking. Dale, the great landlady, arrived with two workmen to replace palm fronds. The roof was a work of art — very geometric and tightly woven. Dale and I had coffee while we watched the fellows work. They could take separate fronds out and replace them with new ones; weaving them back into the roof deftly and quickly. Dale took the trash with her and left me with an intact roof over my head.

#

Sunday, the 6th, we drove to the beach to spend the night. Since we needed gasoline and supplies, decided to go from Cerritos on Monday. The sunset was spectacular: shades of pink, peach, and purple. The clouds over the mountains were huge puffs of dove grey. There was a quarter moon. The beach itself was aglow with all the reflected color. It was like walking on shimmering gold. Both Madrita and Stud curled up outside Tessie for the night. The sea sang her siren song. It was still a mystical, magical setting for me.

#

Next morning was cloudy and cool. The drive to Cabo

was a delight. The desert was green and dotted with pink, yellow, and red flowers that had burst into bloom after the rains. Got all the chores over with as quickly as possible. The sun had broken through the clouds and Cabo was steaming. Did the *panadería,* the new drug store, some shops looking for a better tie-up for Ink on the portal. Got gasoline, picked up dog food for puppies and Ink, then scooted back up the hill and home to cool Todos Santos. Dropped off food for the pups, bread for Adam and Susie. Arrived at the *palapa* around 2:30 p.m. weary and hot. Took a hot tub and a siesta.

# # #

El arrived a few days later distraught over placing the puppies. The five males had been given away quickly, but the three females were a problem. Gabriel was leaving for the University of La Paz soon and El wanted all those pups out of her hair. He had told his mother that if he could find a house with a yard, he'd take all three of the girls with him. He definitely was taking the speckled female who looked like Studly.

I pointed out to El that the Mexicans had not been raised on Walt Disney and animals were just animals. Mentioned that when you're hard-pressed to feed your family, you don't worry much about the dogs. She still agonized.

Finally agreed that if push came to shove, I'd take one of the females. That helped. But I fervently hoped that I'd not have to take on another dog. Didn't feel Ink was ready to share me and really didn't want another dog. Gave El a glass of iced tea and soothed her. Suggested that she get away for a few days and offered to care for all the livestock at the beach.

# # #

I kept trying to find some light rope to tie Ink. There was nothing available in Cabo or Todos Santos. However, looking was informative. Found some nylon shoe strings in a small shop and took them home. Cut the ends off, melted the nylon and tried that. Ink welcomed the soft line since her old lead had gotten very stiff. I looked at that makeshift rope and hoped no chicken strutted by.

While nosing around, I came across the local dentist and walked in. Antonio's office was just a portioned off section of the family living room. There was a TV blaring with a few people sitting and watching. Talked with Antonio about cleaning my teeth and set an appointment for the 16th.

#

Spanish classes started the 15th with Book Three of *Curso Intensivo*. I was happy to go back to class. I knew I was making progress because all the children told me they could understand me, and the kids tell the truth. We were meeting at the garden nursery which Dale and her husband owned. I understood why my yard was so lovely when I saw that well-stocked store. There were now only five students attending.

#

I met El at the post office. We had fish tacos at Pilar's. She asked if I had been serious when I offered to come and care for the livestock. I assured her I'd be happy to be at the beach. She said she wanted to go over to the Gulf side and would like to leave on the 17th. I told her the only restriction was that she must stay away until Sunday.

#

My appointment with the dentist was for 10 a.m. I was on time, but Antonio was 35 minutes late. He apologized and led me into the office. I looked at the equipment and recaptured my youth. He had a big orange drill, an orange spitting sink, and an old dental chair; what dentists in the US used when I was a kid. Antonio worked skillfully. My teeth were a challenge. They had not been cleaned for the entire year I was on the road. He scraped and scraped for an hour, then suggested that I come back tomorrow to finish. I explained that I was to go Cerritos. Asked if he would mind Ink coming along so that we could go on out to the beach from the office. *No problema.*

# # #

That evening there was a full lunar eclipse. Todos Santos was the best viewing area in the Baja. I sat on the portal with my binoculars and watched while I listened to a full explanation on the radio in Spanish. Called over to Elisa and the family to come and view the hiding moon through the binoculars. They had never used binoculars and liked that close up view.

I told them I'd be going out to Cerritos until Sunday to care for the animals while *mi amiga* took a trip. They assured me they would watch over the *palapa*.

# # #

Arrived at the dentist's at 10 a.m. Antonio was waiting. He looked a bit unsettled by my big, black dog. I eased his apprehension with, *"está muy amistosa."* Ink gave him a kiss, then settled in the corner and caused no trouble.

Antonio worked another hour and a half on my filthy teeth and finished the job. For all his labors, he charged me $30.00. We thanked him, and, after one stop at Castro's for canned dog food, arrived at Cerritos a little past noon. El was still packing. I got instructions on feeding the three puppies and two kittens. Ink, Madrita, and Stud walked with me on the beach. When we returned El had left.

# # #

In spite of no market for female dogs, the girls were delightful. They were weaned and ate regular food. Knew they were to stay in their pen, and did just that until I came to let them out for a romp. I had parked down from the barracks in a grove of trees so that I could watch over my charges. Madrita and Stud joined us. I fed everyone dinner, put the puppies to bed for the night and we adults took a long, relaxing stroll on the beach at sunset.

# # #

Was up before the sun on Friday morning. Had coffee and enjoyed the sunrise. Then, it was time for the breakfast round for the pups. I had breakfast and fed the kittens. Let the pups out for some playtime. Thought again what a pity the Mexican people didn't want any female dogs.

Gabriel had named the girls. The one he was keeping was Santee — she looked like Stud, but was more aloof. Bear was going to be big. She loved Ink but Ink did not reciprocate. Dulcinea was most like Madrita and was my favorite. We let them play till mid-morning. They were intelligent, very willing to please, and a joy. I found myself thinking that having one of Madrita's pups wouldn't be all that bad. Ink did not share my feeling. Took the adults and we all had a refreshing swim. The water was warm and soothing.

Gave pups lunch and another romp. They gave Madrita lots of room. She would not tolerate them trying to suckle any longer. Put the girls in for a siesta and we did the same. More playtime in late afternoon. Managed the dinner round for six dogs and two kittens, more romping and then bedtime for the puppies. The kittens just roamed around the grounds and I didn't worry about them. Finished the day with a sunset walk on the beach.

# # #

Saturday morning, the puppies came running down to Tessie. When they heard me, they pushed over the barrier and headed for the food. Got the livestock squared away and went for a walk. When we got back, Gabriel had arrived. He had much to do before University started, so

I left him to his chores and went for a swim. I took care of feeding the animals. Gabriel watered plants, packed, and played with the pups. After we settled the animals for the night, Gabriel joined me for dinner in Tessie. He still insisted that he could manage all three of the pups. I told him that was more trouble than he needed. We visited and finally hung it up about ten.

# # #

Sunday morning, Gabriel was walking the pups when I woke. Since I knew we would just sit and visit, I ate, then took Madrita, Studly, and Ink for a walk. We were way down the beach when I noticed the dogs nosing something close to the cliff. Walked over to see what they had found. It was a dead goat. She had been tethered and must have fallen from the cliff. What I noticed was the black nylon cord round her neck. She was very dead and decomposing, but I held my breath and got that cord off. It was a perfect tie up for Ink on the portal. I chided myself for doing such a thing. Questioned if I had been away from civilization too long. However, the cord was just what we needed and I knew the poor goat didn't mind.

El was home when we got back. We had a short visit. She was more relaxed — happy she had taken a few days away. I packed up and headed for the *palapa*. Unloaded Tess, brushed Ink, and tied the new cord to the post. It was perfect.

# # #

That evening, Hermalinda brought a visitor to the *palapa*. Jose was a school teacher in Cabo San Lucas. We had tea and a good visit as he spoke excellent English. He asked a thought provoking question, "Barbara, why do you travel alone?" I had to think about that for a few minutes and was able to define my preference for solitary travel.

"First, I have total freedom to stop and look at whatever

I choose; to spend time wherever I choose. Second, and most importantly — since I have no one except Ink, I reach out to those around me. I have met so many wonderful people and heard so many wonderful stories. If I had a travel companion, we'd talk to each other and I'd not meet all those wonderful people who have made this journey so delightful."

I grinned and added, "Besides, if I had a travel companion, I'd not be free to live here in Barrio San Ignacio, you know."

We talked some more. Hermalinda told Jose she hoped I'd never leave and he said he hoped that I would be in the *palapa* for a long time.

I smiled and said, *"¿Quién sabe?"*

# # #

These were the hazy, lazy days of summer. The prevailing winds had turned more southerly and we had more humidity. Good days for loafing and taking long siestas. Life went on, but at an ever-slower pace. The kids stopped often, Spanish classes continued and I was receiving letters from all my friends in Las Cruces offering assistance on moving the car. In a way I wanted to see everyone, and in a way I didn't want to make the effort. Did not push my decision as I knew it would all work out.

# # #

Mirta and Hermalinda invited me to a dance in the plaza. At first I said I didn't think so, but then reconsidered. It was a wonderful opportunity to join the festivities, rather than sitting on the portal and listening to that great music echoing through the village.

Mirta's husband drove us in his pick-up truck. He then went home to baby-sit Jorgito and Lula. Mirta was an independent sort and had that husband well-trained.

The band was great. Lots of salsa music and lots of

dancing by these joyous people. I, of course, could not sit still and joined everyone else. No need for a partner, no need for anything but the joy of dancing. Everyone danced. As I was gliding round the plaza, I thought — if everyone in the United States, including me, would get rid of half their stuff and dance twice as much, we'd all be happier.

In spite of worrying that I had made an ass of myself, I had a delightful evening with the girls. Found that my status in the Barrio had risen, when all learned that I loved to dance as much as they. Mirta and Hermalinda invited me to join them often and I danced my way through many balmy, starlit nights on the plaza.

# # #

One Saturday, some of my little girls asked if I'd like to go with them to the *presa.* Go we did! Down the hill, clambering along the canal, through the *huerta,* and finally to the *presa.* The *presa* was a lange pond used for irrigation. There were all kinds of colorful fish darting around. A group of boys were swimming. I took Ink's lead off and in she went. Some of the boys weren't sure about this big, black dog joining them. My girls yelled, *"No tengan miedo. Está muy amistosa."* The boys decided Ink was okay. She was a good swimmer and quite at home in the pond with them. We sat and enjoyed the coolness and the ripe smell of all the growth around the *presa.* Got home about noon, tired and hot but grateful for the kids' invitation.

# # #

After lunch, I mopped the *palapa,* got the clean wash from the line, and took a siesta. When we went for our evening walk, the sky was a sickly yellow and it was strangely still. Took a bath while dinner was cooking. It was then the winds started to howl and the electricity went out. I lit candles, used batteries in the tape deck, and had a romantic dinner.

By this time, the winds were growling and shrieking. Ink came in from the portal without an invitation. I had curled up in bed, when the rain started. The winds continued to shriek and the rainfall grew violent. The heavens had opened up!

By three in the morning, the *palapa* was leaking like a sieve. Ink had joined me on the bed. As I sat there listening to nature's fury, I told her I thought we were in the midst of a hurricane. I sat there perfectly safe, amazed by all the water and wind. Worried about El at the beach and all the people in the lowlands.

Came the dawn. I waded through big puddles in the *palapa* and fixed coffee. Even the roosters did not crow that morning. The winds had abated, but rain was falling steadily. My worst leak was around the main post of the ceiling on which I hung hats and purses. Everything was soaked, but not damaged. We got lots of water through the screens. There was nothing that wouldn't dry, if and when the rain stopped.

Dale called through and confirmed my feeling that we had, indeed, had a hurricane. It was Kiko. It had smashed into Baja at Todos Santos and swept across the peninsula hitting La Paz with all its fury.

A little later Zulima called to see if I was all right. Elisa came over to check on me. She asked if I had been afraid. I was not frightened, just energized and fascinated. Kiko was the best *chubasco* I had ever experienced.

Rain was still falling, but easing up. It finally stopped around 4 p.m. About five, Ink and I took a walk to survey the damage. Our world was soaked. Not much of a problem with flooding here on top of the hill, but on the *ejido* land the force of the water running down hills was evident: lots of erosion and lots of sand piled up. Saw

Life in Barrio San Ignacio

Mario and he told me he had put some boards over his windows. His cinder block *casa* was drier than my *palapa*. On that Sunday, no one was dry in Todos Santos.

# # #

Monday was a day at home. I was catching mice by the droves. Had three traps set and was exterminating about six a day with peanut butter as the snare. Dale had told me to flush the dead mice down the toilet as it was good for the septic system. I could dump those pesky mice into the toilet without a qualm and reset traps. But then, I could take nylon tethers from dead goat's necks, too. Oh, if my friends could see me now!

# # #

Tuesday dawned sunny and humid. Left Ink to guard the *palapa* and set out for Spanish class. Made it down the road which was more rutted than before Kiko. Got to the bridge and — it was gone. Whoa! There was a small barricade, but no bridge. That charming little *presa* where the kids had taken me on the previous Saturday morning had become a raging torrent. All the water flowing down the mountains had flooded the entire *huerta* and wiped out the bridge plus a lot of crops.

I was sitting there wondering how to get into town or if I was stranded in Barrio San Ignacio until they built a new bridge. About that time, Julian the painter, came barreling down the hill in his VW "thing". He motioned for me to follow him. It was a wild drive, over washed out roads, through puddles the size of lakes, all at fifty miles an hour. We finally came out on the main highway north of town. Got to Spanish class more than a little breathless.

Everyone had stories to tell of the encounter with Kiko. The important news was that no one had been killed in our area. Learned that the highway was closed and that La Paz had been hard hit. There would be no supplies coming into

Todos Santos for a few days.

El arrived at the nursery during Spanish class. I was relieved to see she had weathered the storm. She said it was bad, but the Airstream held its ground. Mentioned that the beach was a disaster. I told her I'd try and get out to Cerritos soon.

# # #

The clean-up started. I knew I'd be using a long detour until the bridge was rebuilt. The weather was horrible — humid, muggy, and buggy. Everyone was sweating and swatting. I continued catching mice. Think they had all come inside to escape the storm. But on the winds of the *chubasco,* a multitude of butterflies had been swept in. They were a delight: all sizes, shapes, and colors flitting around the yard. I concentrated on those butterflies, rather than the damn mice.

The barrio was digging out. Neighbors were helping each other. Some of the men were raking the road and filling in the ruts. I took two rakes, a shovel, and a wheelbarrow I had in the storage shed down to them. Not sure Dale would have approved, but the men were grateful and returned everything.

# # #

Wednesday, Dale sent Juan Louis and Adolfo to clean up the grounds. I decided to stay home and oversee the yard work. There were broken branches everywhere. They cleaned and raked the yard and driveway, tightened up the clothes lines, trimmed the bougainvillea, fixed the fence, and took the trash. I cleaned all the shelves in the *palapa* of mouse droppings.

# # #

Thursday, we drove out to Cerritos through still flowing *vados.* Sand was piled high in some spots, but we made it through. The beach was a disaster. Wood and flotsam of all kinds washed on shore and lots of erosion. Mother Nature can still make us realize how hopelessly inadequate we are to deal with her fury. I couldn't believe the mounds of wood on the shore. Wondered where those logs had come from.

El was fine. She fixed lunch and we talked late. I was still vacillating over making the trip to the states. El discerned that I really didn't want to do it; however, I pointed out that it was my responsibility — even though I hated to go.

El related a local myth which was prophetic. It seems the nationals who bought Los Pedritos RV park had pushed the sale. Some of the elders of the family who owned the land did not want to sell. One of the *abuelos* walked down to the operation one day and was so displeased with what they were doing, he placed a curse on the park. He predicted that the rains would demolish it. And Hurricane Kiko did. The park was in the middle of a wide *vado* and the waters stormed down that arroyo and wiped out everything but the restaurant which was on higher ground.

We got home at dusk. I had turned on just one light when I glanced across the room. What looked like a big snake was slithering across the rug. I just stood there transfixed. Turned on another light and moved closer. No snake, thank God, but a line of ants about three inches wide parading on the white rug. I sprayed heavily and cursed heavily. Seemed I had gotten the mouse problem in hand and now ants were taking over. Killed all of them and swept them up. Hopped into bed wondering what would be next. Ah, life in the tropics.

# # #

September began muddy, humid, and buggy. My neighbors had always been kind and friendly, but I sensed a subtle change. Now that I had weathered the hurricane, they were more accepting of this strange woman among them.

I felt I was traveling light in the camper, but I had a hammer, a flashlight, screwdrivers, and wrenches. None of my neighbors had any of these things and would now ask me to borrow them. I lent them gladly. In spite of warnings that I'd never get them back or they would come back broken, it was not so.

I learned that communal life, where no one had many possessions, was one in which you all shared what you had. So, when Jorge yelled over for the use of tools, I lent them willingly. When the boys stopped to use the foot pump to inflate flat tires on their bikes, I was happy to lend it.

In turn, when I needed a machete to trim trees and shrubs, Jorge was so delighted that I asked him, he honed that machete to a fine edge and brought it to me.

The children arrived almost daily with *flores*. It was all they had to give. When I told them I liked fish, they brought jars of darting colorful fish from the *presa*. The custom of sharing was strong and they were generous. I enjoyed helping with the loan of a few things. I had so many items my neighbors couldn't afford — aspirin, rubbing alcohol, Band-aids — things I took for granted — that many in the barrio didn't have money to buy. My *palapa* became a small supply center. I found the sharing custom pleasing.

# # #

More adults were coming to visit. The days started early, but the evenings were for socializing. The ladies came to call. I felt honored and we would sit and smile and try to talk. I learned they didn't feel free to leave without some sign from me that it was all right. Solved that impasse by standing and saying there were chores I had to do. I would thank them for coming and they would leave with smiles and *"hasta luegos."* After some sessions, my brain felt like a soft taco. But it was wonderful to know that I was accepted.

# # #

Along with the neighbors' acceptance of us, the dogs also started to visit. There was an assortment: Jorge and Elisa had a mutt named Salchicha who looked like he had been assembled from spare dog parts. He would come and wait on the portal in the evening then join Ink and me for our walks. A really ugly dog, but just as sweet as he could be. Jorge and Elisa acquired another terrier-type mutt who was cute. He also joined us for evening walks. Both of them would try to steal Ink's food, but she learned to stand her ground. I would give them a hand-out from time to time. Mirna and Juanito's male dog, Indio, was alpha dog in the barrio. He was muscular and big and dominated the herd. Ramon had the only other female dog around. She looked like a mop and was called Perla. When she came into heat, they had a novel way of protecting her. Ramon would carry her up to the roof of their concrete house and tie her in the shade of the *pela*. All the males congregated down below, but could not get to Perla. There was a lot of fighting and frustration, but no breeding. It was poor Salchicha who always got torn up in those frays. He'd come and sit on our portal trying to figure it out — looking beaten and forlorn. But, the heat would end, Perla would be brought down from the roof and all returned to normal.

# # #

My neighbors to the south were the wealthy ones in the barrio. They had an automatic washer that had never been installed and leveled properly. With the low water pressure, it took ages for the washer to fill. Most of the time it went out of balance on the spin cycle and walked across the room. I could watch and hear all this from my door. Wanted to help level that machine, but thought better of offering.

# # #

Elisa and her girls did not smoke at home. They'd come in the evening and we'd all have tea and a cigarette together. Mirta told me her father never knew any of them smoked. Elisa had been smoking for twenty years, but Jorge never knew. These women handled their men so adeptly and well. They were the ones in charge, but their husbands never knew.

The more I observed and listened to the women in the Barrio, the more I knew they ran the show. Granted, the men were swaggering and macho in the public arena, but on the domestic front, the women were in charge and managed everything. They did it with a subtlety and grace that would teach some of the more strident women in our culture a valuable lesson.

This was so obvious to me when El brought a husband-and-wife dental team from La Paz to the *palapa*. They were a handsome couple who were starving and had come over to Todos Santos with fliers to see if they could entice some business. The husband suggested they hand out fliers at the baseball stadium where there was a game in progress. His wife said no way, it was the wives who decided how the money would be spent — no use to bother with the men. This couple had visited relatives in Los Angeles thinking they might move there and earn a living. After being warned to lock everything, to not answer a door, to be careful on the streets, etc., they decided L.A. was no place for them. They'd rather starve in La Paz and know they were safe.

Somehow this division of labor worked well for the Mexican people in the Barrio. I could hear everything in

Life in Barrio San Ignacio

my immediate neighborhood through that thatched roof. I never heard husbands and wives arguing or fighting, I never heard a child being spanked or abused. I never heard any dissension of any kind. No one griped about neighbors, dogs, chickens, or anything. Something worked very well for these families — my guess would be love and respect.

# # #

I was still agonizing about going to Las Cruces to move my car. Knew I didn't want to leave my little Eden, but knew it was my responsibility. Everyone in the Barrio knew I was planning a trip and the wish lists were lengthening each day. All my neighbors had something they wanted me to bring back from the States.

When I got a letter from a couple in Cruces offering to move the car down to their property in the valley, it was a blessing. After much deliberation, I decided not to go to the States. It meant a lot of phone calls back and forth. The Carpenters assured me that moving the car was no trouble, Berchie said the plan sounded good to her. Many of my friends expressed disappointment at my not making an appearance, but, I was relieved and grateful to the Carpenters that I didn't have to go.

One great learning experience was my ability to make plane reservations and be understood in Spanish. I had called La Paz for information on flights. The clerk answered to my query, "¿Se habla ingles?" with "Un poco". So with her speaking *un poco* English and my speaking *un poco* Spanish, we finally got it all together. I never was sure whether my reservation was confirmed from Tucson to El Paso, but no matter. I canceled the whole trip.

# # #

School stated early September and my mornings were more relaxed. However, the children stopped on their way home and reported on their school day. Todos Santos had a high school which was unusual for the Baja. The children were getting a good, basic education.

Jorgito, Mirta's son, started first grade that year. Jorgito would come in and sit at the counter and practice; *uno, dos, tres,* over and over again. At times, he would get to *cinco* or *seis* before he had to start over, but he kept practicing. We had a crazy game which we played. He would arrive saying, *"Buenos dias. ¿Cómo está?"* I would respond, *"Bien, ¿y usted?"* Then, Jorgito would respond, *"Bien, ¿y usted?"* and I'd say again, *"Bien, ¿y usted?"* We'd do this until we both burst into laughter. Lula, his sister, was at the *palapa* often, too. But it was Jorgito with his flashing dark eyes and ready smile who stole my heart. Perhaps it was because I had sons. He was very special.

My two favorite girls were Mirna and Cariña. They were both neighbors, constantly together, and about nine. Mirna was a study in sepia and beautiful. She lived on the other side of Elisa and Jorge. Her father was the manager at Bancomer. She and her older brother, Juanito, had 21 cousins — all of whom were in the *palapa* looking at the *baño* at one time or another. Cariña looked like an Indian and was always in trouble. She dropped everything or broke everything she touched. I could empathize since I had had the same trouble when I was her age.

These two young girls were at the *palapa* constantly. They loved to come over while I was fixing dinner and watch me cook. I always offered them a taste and they liked that. They were amazed that I often cooked *frijoles.* Guess they thought gringas ate only steak.

I never lacked company. In fact, it was one of the hardest adjustments — constant company. No one seemed to think I should be alone. I had to fight for privacy. I would have to close the door and shutters and take a quiet break from time to time.

# # #

Since I had canceled the States trip, I mentioned to El that I wanted to see about having Madrita spayed. All the puppies were gone. El had found homes for the two females and Gabriel had only one dog to care for in La Paz. It seemed time to get the old girl some freedom. El was elated. She didn't want the chore of getting rid of another litter. She was going to La Paz and suggested stopping at the vet's for a sedative for Madrita. Neither of us knew if she had ever been in a car. El offered to go along and help with this undertaking.

On the fifth of September, I met El in Todos Santos, since she did not know how to negotiate the detour. El parked her pick-up at Stewart's. She had given Madrita the sedative and old gal was on cloud nine. We put her into the camper on the bed and headed for La Paz with a very docile dog. I had left Ink to guard the *palapa*.

Wenseslau, the veterinarian, was a wonderful man. He was so impressed that I wanted to spay Madrita, he cut the price of the operation to $20.00. Not only that, he allowed us to watch the entire process. Wenseslau talked as he worked away. He said he thought Madrita was between eight and ten years old. When he mentioned that her liver was enlarged, we all laughed over her being a *borracha* when she was young.

El and I made it clear that we wanted a total hysterectomy for this old girl. The usual method of spaying in Mexico is to remove the tubes, but leave the ovaries. That way the female has a heat, but will not breed. It makes for the total chaos of any bitch in heat; all the males gather and carry on. No way did we want that for Madrita.

The operation went well and we were back on the road by noon. Did nothing in La Paz but see about the spaying.

El asked if I wanted to keep Madrita at the *palapa* for a few days. Much as I loved that old gal, I declined, knowing she'd be happier at home on the beach. El did not mind tending to her. I assured her I'd be out in a few days to see how the patient fared. We loaded Madrita, still very woozy, into the pickup. Had a hug, then I went back home by way of the detour. Felt happy about this deed. Knew Madrita was no longer at the mercy of her pheromones and there would be fewer unwanted puppies in the Baja.

# # #

Dale sensed that I felt a bit let-down about canceling my trip. Even though I was relieved, I had gotten wound up to make the journey and was now having a downer. She called and invited me to go to La Paz for the day. Dale had business chores, but suggested that I browse and we'd have lunch together. I accepted gratefully.

I wandered around downtown La Paz. Visited the major department store, Dorian's, and found panties which I desperately needed. It was a large well-stocked store with escalators and all the amenities. They carried a big Sony line and I bought a new tape deck. This was the third one I had acquired since I started traveling. It was the same model I had bought in Las Cruces in January, but $10 cheaper. I then walked and wandered in and out of shops along the *malecon*. Got into lots of trouble. The ladies were always asking if I owned a dress. Most of the women in the Barrio wore dresses, no slacks. As a matter of fact, I did not own a dress at the time and decided that I should have one. Bought two everyday cottons and one fancy dress. Knew it would please my neighbors.

The bathing suit I bought was for no one's eyes. It was the skimpiest suit I had ever had in my life; just some straps and not much else. Not one that I would wear in public, but I knew the dogs at the beach would never tell.

Life in Barrio San Ignacio 135

Dale had given explicit instructions on finding the restaurant. It was a long hike up the hill, but I had no trouble locating the Hong Kong Restaurant. Yes, we had lunch at a Chinese restaurant on the second floor of Moorish type building in the heart of La Paz. How cosmopolitan can one get?

Dale was flying to Canada for a wedding the end of the month. Over lunch she said she had found a dress she thought would be appropriate. She asked if I'd come to the shop and give my opinion. So, I got to visit another charming shop in La Paz. It was quality and the dress Dale had chosen was lovely. With my blessing, she bought it. We then dashed into a drug store and I, at last, found dental floss. There was none to be had in Todos Santos. The excursion lifted my spirits greatly. Thanked Dale for a fun time in the big city and told her I was glad I had not made the trip to the States.

# # #

Ink and I saw Mario and his pup, Sultan, occasionally when we walked. We would sit on a big rock by the road and watch the sun set into the Pacific. Mario continued to encourage my endeavors with Spanish. I had learned by this time that I could comprehend some people better than others. Mario was easy to talk with and that gave me added confidence.

He came to call one Saturday, all dressed up. I invited him in. About that time Mirna and Cariña arrived. I served Mario a cup of tea and gave the girls some juice. We were all chatting away when Mario told the girls he thought I should marry him. Oh, God! I responded, *"No quiero casarme con nadie, ¡nunca!"* Mirna and Cariña both clapped. This turn of events with Mario disturbed me. I didn't think that I had led him to believe I was interested in more than a friendship, but here he was thinking of marriage.

\# \# \#

Drove out to Cerritos to check on Madrita. The old gal was doing really well; the incision was healing nicely. She seemed to realize that she was free of having any more litters. She had a new lease on life. Stud was her constant companion. They hung out together. Madrita would need his youth to catch food when there was no one around to feed them. I was sure Stud would share.

\# \# \#

The bugs were atrocious. I was told it was *"bo-bo"* season. These pesky bugs swarmed in a cloud around everyone and everything, getting into eyes, noses, and ears, especially if there was no breeze. Dale told me the children often had eye infections from those pesky little things. Evenings when we walked, there would be a cloud hovering around Ink and I was constantly swatting. I took my straw hat and sprayed the brim with insect repellent and it deterred the little devils. Then, started putting some spray down Ink's back and our walks became tolerable. Since everyone wore hats, I walked around the barrio with spray can in hand. Saying, *"Mira,"* I'd spray the outside and inside brim and explain, *"No más bo-bos."* Then I'd spray their hats, if they consented. Relieved a lot of neighbors from the agony of those pesky bugs.

\# \# \#

El was taking a one day junket to some ranch in the mountains and asked if I'd come to Cerritos and look after the dogs. I was ready to escape the barrio for a while and agreed. Friday evening, pulled onto my sacred point of land. Madrita and Stud joined us immediately. Fed those two and Ink a gourmet meal, then sat and watched the sunset. El came down and said she'd be leaving early. I told her we'd let Gilly out and care for her. There was no one at Cerritos. I relished a quiet day.

Saturday morning, after watching a gorgeous sunrise, slipped into the new bathing suit and we walked down the beach. Stud and Ink would romp and dig for crabs, sprint in and out of the water, but Madrita and I strolled slowly with her licking my hand from time to time. It was fun watching the youngsters play, but we preferred a slower pace. Madrita sensed her new freedom. The burden from litters was over.

I loved the barrio and all the people, but it was akin to living in a fish bowl in the middle of a three ring circus at times. I savored the serenity of Cerritos. The beach was still littered with reminders of Kiko. I found a large piece of driftwood shaped with a goat's head and a long serpent body. Knew it would look great in my *baño,* so loaded it in Tessie.

With the heavy rains, the field next to the campground had become a vast lake. It was teeming with water fowl of all kinds. I spent some time with the binoculars watching geese and ducks skimming over the water.

El got back late Saturday night stating that she was exhausted from conversing in Spanish all day. I welcomed her to the club.

After two nights of solitude, I returned to the *palapa* ready for another round of barrio life. Had some sunburn on parts of my body that had never seen sun before, thanks to the new suit.

# # #

Dale planned to drive to California, leave the car for some repair work, then fly to Canada for the wedding and family reunion. As is the custom, she offered to take mail and post it in the States. I was happy to be able to send checks and mail along since it shortened the time by at least a week. So sat and typed a bunch of letters and business items that had to be handled. We had Spanish on the 26th and then no classes until Dale returned. Rosalie, one of the students, was driving as far as California with Dale. She'd pick up all my mail at Stewart's on the 28th. Mary Lou was another class member. She and Charles had moved to Todos Santos from Taos, New Mexico and were kindred spirits. They had a big, rambling house in town with a veranda surrounding it and cages of birds hanging everywhere. Mary Lou was a great cook. Charles was a painter. I enjoyed them and their friendship.

# # #

Ink and I were returning from our sunset walk when Jorge called to me to come, sit, and visit. Boy, I knew I had arrived! And, we could converse. Jorge, although he seemed so gruff and patriarchal, was a pussy-cat under that stern exterior. Think he wanted to see why the women in the family enjoyed coming to the *palapa* so often. It was a nice visit, even tho' Jorge told me Mario was loco. I went home feeling I had passed the test.

Next evening as we were returning from our walk, Ink pounced on one of Jorge's prize chickens and scared it to death. The chicken died of fright. I apologized and offered to pay for it. Jorge was more than a little miffed and I was sure I was back at square one. However, Elisa and the girls assured me that Jorge would forgive me and that I had made a conquest.

# # #

The kids had been hellish and I was refusing to let them come into the *palapa*. I went out to the yard the last Saturday of the month intending to rake and clean up leaves. Well, those hellish kids all arrived and all helped me with the work. In fact, they were standing in line for turns on who would rake and who would empty the wheelbarrow. The boys did those chores while the girls swept the portal and gazebo. Now how can you stay angry with such willing helpers? The yard was cleaned in two hours and we all had cookies and juice in the gazebo.

# # #

October weather was perfect — warm sunny days and cool nights. The humidity had lessened and life was tolerable. On the second, Elisa came over to tell me her brother in La Paz had died. She went on to say that she had another brother in Mexicali and, of course, Mario here in Todos Santos. She and Jorge did not go for the funeral. Here in the Baja, the bodies are buried within 24 hours as there are no embalming facilities.

Each afternoon friends and relatives gathered at Jorge and Elisa's *casa* for a small memorial service. This continued for nine days and sent the deceased on his way. I would hear singing from their house and thought it was a nice tribute. But then, death and dying is acceptable in the Baja.

# # #

I met Jim at the Stewart's. Learned that he was my nearest gringo neighbor. He lived about two miles from me — across the *ejido* land and closer to the sea. Seemed an interesting man. His sailboat sank in the Gulf one Halloween night. It was a total loss and Jim couldn't afford another boat, so settled in Todos Santos. He had lived in Nova Scotia, so welcomed my views on the Maritimes and the rest of my travels. Jim invited me down to watch the sunset from his balcony. We struck up a nice friendship. Jim would stop at the *palapa,* I would walk over to his house. We always had lots to discuss. Jim read avidly and was more current on the gossip in the gringo community than I. He would fill me in with his own views. I found that most of the *Norteamericanos* were still playing the same games — my *palapa* is bigger than yours, did you hear about — and I found it dull, so I spent more time with my neighbors in the Barrio. Still, the grapevine worked exceedingly well.

# # #

The first week-end of October, Todos Santos celebrated with a fiesta for its patron saint, Pilar. I asked Jim if he would accompany me. It didn't seem proper to go alone. Jim was happy to go and we set out on Sunday evening to view the celebration. I wore the spiffy rose dress that I had bought in La Paz and a straw hat. Jorge yelled over — *"que bonita"*. Then Mario came out of the drive with thunder in his eyes saying his heart was broken. Jim inquired if he was going to be stabbed.

We parked at Charles and Mary Lou's house and walked up to the festival which was set up on the main plaza across from the Catholic church. There were booths laden with wares and food. A great band, and carnival rides including a ferris wheel, were set up on the vacant lot below the church and next to Hotel California. It was a time to meet and greet since everyone attended.

Even the governor of Baja Sur was there. He arrived in a large bus and dedicated the new Pemex station and the paving of the main street. Until it was paved, the only non-dirt road in town was Route 19. I watched the slow progress on the street and thought it would never be finished on time. Somehow, it was. The workers must have toiled all night because it was far from done on Friday when I was in town. Jim, Charles, Mary Lou and I had a lovely evening — eating, visiting, dancing, and talking with everyone. The one sour note was Mario lurking in the background. We took our leave about 11 p.m. just as the fiesta queen was being crowned.

# # #

With the afternoon services, Mario was at Jorge and

Elisa's. Sultan, his pup, arrived at my door in wretched shape. He was covered with sores and ticks, his legs swollen and bleeding, and he looked like he was starving. I didn't even want to touch the poor beast, but he had come to me seeking help and I had to try and heal him. I gave him some food, sprayed all the sores with disinfectant, and put a mat outside for him to sleep on. We didn't want that mangy dog in the *palapa*. The kids would kick at him, and try to chase him away. I wouldn't let them abuse this poor creature. Ink and I agreed we had to help, so we nursed Sultan and he improved.

I spoke to Mario about his sick pup and he just shrugged and said, *"Muy enfermo."* He was deliberately starving Sultan. After Mario's atrocious behavior at the fiesta, and now this episode with the pup, I began to think I didn't want to associate with him. Elisa looked at the dog and said, *"muriendo"* suggesting that I not bother. And, this is their view of dealing with sick dogs. These people were not into the Disney syndrome. Dogs were just that; either *"viviendo"* or *"muriendo."* I could understand their reasoning and yet could not let a dog starve to death. Ink and I nursed Sultan and put out a lot of energy, but in the end, he died. I felt really bad, but took comfort in knowing he had had some TLC before he bowed out. I'm sure my neighbors thought I was crazy to bother with that animal, but it's a different world view. Surely, they also wondered why I was so good to Ink. Dogs were just dogs, nothing more to them.

# # #

Jorge and Elisa's four daughters came home for five days the middle of October. Mercedes from Ensenada, Carmela from La Paz, and Mirta and Hermalinda who both lived in Todos Santos. It was delightful having them there. The neighborhood was filled with laughter and lots of activity. Both Mercedes and Carmela had babies and would come over to visit with those darling children. It was a loving family reunion and I was pleased to be a small part of it. I would be reading at night and listening to the sounds of happy talk, guitar playing, and lots of laughter. I offered to take some photos of the entire family and they were so appreciative. They all posed in the palapa and we had quite a photography session.

# # #

November started on a high note. Mark called saying he and Lois would arrive in La Paz on the 17th and be able to stay only one week. It didn't seem long enough, but I was ecstatic that the kids were coming.

Ink and I made a trip to La Paz on the second with a map in hand to do a run-through. I didn't want to drive the kids around in circles as I usually did, since I always got lost. I had bought a city map and was determined to find my way through that city.

Tried for the airport, and found it on the first attempt. Then, with more studying of the map, drove into town and stopped at La Posada, a lovely old Inn on the bay. Since Mark and Lois did not get into La Paz until 5:15 p.m., I made reservations there for the night. Knew I would not drive the highway after dark and endanger us. Besides, the kids would love a night at La Posada. This old Inn had a great restaurant that served meals beside the pool. Soon enough to get to Todos Santos the following day. Ink and I had lunch by the pool after looking at the rooms,

Stopped and picked up supplies at CCC and then out of town without being lost once.

# # #

Got back to Todos Santos in time to see some of the celebration that accompanied the day of the dead (*El dia de los muertos*). On this day, the people take food, flowers,

Life in Barrio San Ignacio

and gifts and place them on the graves of departed loved ones. Many families carried candles and walked solemnly through town and out to the cemetery to remember and care for the dead. It was quite touching.

# # #

El flew off to Tucson on the sixth for treatment for her dog, Gilly's, teeth. She had been in for lunch and said she had to help poor Gilly, and Wenseslau in La Paz could not do the work. Thought how different our approach was from the Mexican one of letting them die. We discussed the upcoming visit of my chickies. El offered her tent which I planned to use, if we stayed at Cerritos. Tessie was to be the guest room. Also, El said that she'd keep Ink while I went to the airport.

# # #

Drove out to the beach and fed Madrita and Stud and had a long walk with them, but did not spend the night. My energies were directed to making the kids' visit a memorable one. Cleaned Tessie and the *palapa* since I wanted everything spick and span. Not that the kids would care, but it seemed the thing to do. So my days were full and joyous getting ready for company. My excitement pervaded the barrio. Everyone was stopping to ask about Mark and Lois and offer help.

# # #

El got home from Tucson on the 12th. Gilly's teeth were much improved. She had an amusing tale to tell. Had deplaned at the airport and was waiting for luggage and Gilly's crate. Decided she needed some fresh air and went through a door — only to be pinned to the wall by a group of security agents. As she told it, the door was not marked exit, but she thought it would be all right to step outside and get some fresh air. Not so. Paranoia reigns supreme in the states. We had a great laugh over her experience and decided that she would not make a good mule. She was happy to be home safe and sound at Cerritos.

# # #

In the midst of all my frenzied preparations. Mario yelled at Ink and me one evening on our walk. We sat on our rock by the road for a small visit. And, Mario proposed — marriage. I was taken aback, but touched by this humble man's proposal, ludicrous as it was. Mario pledged his undying love and told me that if I would marry him, he'd build me a kitchen. In his eyes, this was the greatest gift he could give me. Who could ask for more? I reiterated that I was not interested in getting married — ever, but he didn't seem to believe me. Knew I must stop talking to him, since he was encouraged by my friendliness. Then, too, after the episode with Sultan, my feelings had changed. Still, Mario, gave it his best shot.

# # #

On the 16th, I drove out to Cerritos with Ink. El and I had lunch together. I had decided, by this time, to drive the kids home by way of San Juan del Cabo and Cabo San Lucas. Some nice sightseeing for them and the drive north on Route 19 would bring us to the beach to pick up Ink. She was happy to stay with El and the dogs, but it was the first time in 15 months that we had been apart. It was like getting away from the kids when they were young. I felt free as a bird.

# # #

When I left for La Paz, Dale and her fellows were raking the yard of the *palapa*. Elisa yelled over that they'd be waiting for our return. Everyone was looking forward to the visit from Mark and Lois.

Got to La Paz early and checked into our rooms, changed clothes, and stretched out for a short rest. Then on to the airport. The flight was on time and the kids had arrived. Oh Joy!

#

The first thing both of them said to me was, "God, are you ever thin!" I didn't have a scale and never thought of my weight. Just felt wonderful and tan. But the kids couldn't stop commenting on it. Mark started calling me "stick Mother." Finally told them it must be all the dancing in the plaza.

We had our hugs and I welcomed them to the land of mañana. Got the luggage and drove to La Posada. Mark commented on all the traffic. I was used to La Paz and never noticed anymore, but the streets were crowded.

Let the kids get settled and unpacked. They had one bag filled with goodies for me: ribbons for Little Brother, new jazz tapes, and oodles of bath salts and lotions. We took a short walk on the beach. The lights of La Paz were sparkling on the water, the palms were swaying, and it was properly lugubrious.

Dinner poolside was delightful. The fountain was splashing and the stars shining. We had a movable feast. Just sat and grinned at each other a lot. I ran through the schedule for the following morning and they thought the drive around the Cape would be fun. We all turned in early since it had been a long day.

#

I was so glad I had studied that map. We made it out of La Paz in one try and headed south. Stopped at San Jose del Cabo and wandered around while we ate ice cream. Then, on to Cabo. I pointed out the RV park where we had stayed, drove the kids out to the quay, and then we browsed the open air bazaar. Asked if they'd like to stop at my favorite *panadería*. Mark and Lois couldn't resist all those goodies and loaded up a tray. Knew we were going to have enough supplies.

Got to Cerritos about 3:30. Ink and the dogs all greeted us with wagging tails. El was happy to meet my kids. We gave her some goodies from the *panadería*. After a short visit, we headed home.

I was amazed that the neighbors didn't have a marching band out to greet us. Pulled in and everyone descended on us. I had warned my kids it would be busy. They enjoyed meeting all my neighbors. Had dinner quietly since the local kids were on best behavior. Jorge came over with a couple of beers for Mark and seemed to approve of my children. Told Mark and Lois to put toilet paper in the basket. They had already learned this custom at La Posada since it was *de riguor* for the Baja. Then gave them the fifty cent tour. They thought the *palapa* was charming.

Lois and I were out in Tessie making the bed when Mario came staggering into the camper. He was drunk as a skunk. We couldn't even understand him, but he was happy to meet Lois. Mark came out about that time and asked who this drunken man was. I told him Mario wanted to be his future step-father. We finally got him out of Tess and the kids came in and had a beer. I asked them if they'd like to spend some time on the beach and they were in agreement. Hugged good-night with me warning them that the roosters would wake them early. No problem.

# # #

As we were eating breakfast, all the kids arrived with flowers, cucumbers, melons. and big smiles. Think my young ladies were entranced by Mark's blue, blue eyes. Lois could speak some Spanish and got along well. Mark just grinned and said, *"Gracias."* It was all he needed to do. Young Jorge whispered to me that Mark had big muscles.

Got squared away. Let Elisa and Jorge know that we were going out to camp at Cerritos and we headed out for

Life in Barrio San Ignacio

some peace and quiet.

Stayed in the campground under a tree. Francisco came to greet my children and brought us a table and some chairs. Got the tent from El and we were settled in quickly. Way out on the curve of the ocean, two whales sounded. This wasn't the time for whales, but I thought it was a nice gift for the children.

I had told Lois I would do the cooking. I was used to the small quarters in Tessie and she was on vacation. We dined by starlight and listened to the sea. I could see the kids slowly relaxing under the spell of this glorious setting.

# # #

We camped until Thanksgiving Day. Got into town about noon and had fish tacos at Pilar's. Then drove around the town and Mark took pictures. Got home in time for baths before all the kids arrived. Mark took pictures of them and we all took a sunset walk on the desert.

All the *Norteamericanos* were having a dinner at El Molino and I insisted that Mark and Lois meet them. So, back into town and did the rounds at El Molino, but choose to have a quiet dinner at Hotel California. This was our last evening and it had all gone too fast. Felt they were more at ease about their Mom being in a foreign land and knew that I had wonderful people surrounding me. They weren't quite used to cockroaches in the tub and all the bugs, but managed. It was just so good to have them with me, even for a few days.

# # #

Had to get away by nine to get the kids to the airport in time. Let Ink ride along because I knew I'd need her company when Mark and Lois flew away. They said their good-byes to all the neighbors who assured them they would take care of "Barbla," and away we went. Saw them onto the plane and then Ink and I parked along the highway and waved until the plane was out of sight. What a letdown, but what a wonderful, loving visit! We didn't even shop in La Paz, just headed for home with great memories.

Needless to say, I was feeling a bit low. Mirna, Cariña, and Veronica came by just before dark. The girls asked me if I was sad and I said I was. They all hugged me and said, *"Estamos aquí."* I appreciated that.

# # #

The final days of November were cloudy and dismal. They matched my mood. Spent some time in quiet contemplation and rested. I had so enjoyed the visit from my children and was so grateful that they had come to this foreign land. Knew they rested more easily knowing that I was happy here in Barrio San Ignacio and surrounded by loving, caring people. Still, the let-down was bad. A few days of rest and giving thanks for all my blessings, got me back into the swing of life in my cozy barrio. And, I still knew it was where I wanted and needed to be.

# # #

Mark and Lois and I had discussed Christmas while they were with me. I suggested rather than dealing with mailing from Baja, we skip gifts. Their visit was the best present I could have. I preferred to spend money on gifts for all my children in the Barrio. Mark and Lois loved the idea and told me they would let Scot and Juli know. So, I started thinking about that lovely task.

Unlike the U.S. there was no hype to get out there and buy, buy, buy for Christmas before the Pilgrim's landed. It was so refreshing and, to my mind, the way Christmas should be. Not commercial, but rather a time for celebrating the Christ child's birth. It was not until the first week of December that any cards, presents, or even wrapping paper appeared in the stores. How lovely!

# # #

Ink and I made a trip to La Paz on the fourth since I needed supplies from CCC, batteries for my camera, and some time just strolling around. The weather was cool enough that Ink did not mind guarding the camper. I was downtown — walking and looking — when I spotted a small shop with decorations in the window. They were made of straw: colorful stars, wreaths, candy canes, and little angels. Went in and had a great time choosing some decorations and lights for a tree — which I did not have. The choices were extensive and quite reasonable and I bought a whole lot of cute, little decorations and a string of lights. Was not sure where I'd find a tree, but that didn't stop me. Wandered some more and found batteries for the camera. Then, did a good marketing at CCC. They had Lender's Bagels and Philly Cream Cheese. I considered it a special holiday present. Treated Ink to lunch at La Posada by the pool. Seemed like eons since the kids and I had sat by the pool, but it had only been a little over two weeks.

# # #

I gave a lot of thought to presents for my barrio children and knew that each age group should have the same gift. I did play favorites with Jorgito and Lula, but they were extra special.

On the 13th, I left Ink at Cerritos with El and headed for Cabo in quest of gifts. Ended up buying Oaxaca yarn dolls for all my girls in the 8 to 10 category. These boy and girl dolls came in assorted colors and were joined by a yarn string. I was sure the girls would like them because they always admired my dolls from Oaxaca which I had hung in the *palapa*. Found small metal cars for the boys, an extra big truck for Jorgito, and a cuddly doll for Lula. Then hedged my bets with some Disney pencils and two pounds of M & M's. Even found wrapping paper.

Didn't get home until 6 p.m. but Elisa, Mirta, and Hermalinda were over in a minute. They were as excited as kids with my plan to play Santa and just had to see what I had bought. We all had some tea while viewing the goodies. They approved heartily and told me I was going to make a lot of children happy.

# # #

I had an old wicker basket by the door; one that had washed up on the beach and El brought to me. Each evening, after I was sure there would be no visitors, I would wrap a few more gifts and place them in the basket. Believe me, the kids did a mental count each time they were in the *palapa*. As the basket got fuller, their eyes grew bigger.

I found a small living Norfolk Island pine at Dale's nursery and put it in a bucket with Christmas paper around the outside. Placed the tree on the table in the living area. Had only one string of small, blinking lights but it was adequate. With all the straw ornaments, the tree looked festive. It was the first time I had had a tree in five years and I enjoyed it. The kids were enthralled with *mi arbolito*. Each time they came in the afternoon, I'd light the tree and they'd all applaud. Such fun!

# # #

There were dances every night on the plaza followed by a fireworks display. Lots of festivities. My joy was diminished because Ink got very, very sick. She would not eat nor wag her tail. For two days she just lolled on her pillow. Knew we had to make a trip to the vet in La Paz. On the 18th, a rainy morning, we set out to see Wenseslau. I worried about *vados* flowing, but there was only one and a track had been made around it.

Wenseslau examined my puny gal. Told me she had a high fever and gave her a shot of penicillin. We were to

Life in Barrio San Ignacio 151

come back to his office at 4 p.m. He closed from 1 until 4 for siesta. So there we were in La Paz. Drove down to the beach, but Ink didn't want to play. So used the time to find oil and a filter for Tessie, got a bite of lunch and we returned to Wenseslau at four. He took Ink's temperature again and the fever had not subsided. All he could tell me was she had an infection. With that, he asked if I had ever given an injection. My God, I had never given an injection to anyone or anything at anytime in my life. He, in his realistic way, said I'd have to learn how or make the 100 mile trip to La Paz each day for a series of penicillin shots for Ink. Then, he proceeded to show me how easy it all was.

I left with penicillin vials for five days of shots. Wenseslau told me I could buy syringes at the local *farmacia* in Todos Santos and that I needed a thermometer. I was to take Ink's temperature on Thursday morning and call him. If it was normal, which would be 38.5 degrees C, the crisis was over. If she still had fever, we would have to get back to La Paz for some blood tests. This was a little overwhelming, but I knew that I'd do what I had to do for my dog. The two shots she had gave Ink a boost, but she still did not eat when we got home.

Next morning, I got syringes and a thermometer at the *farmacia*. Luckily, saw El in town and asked if she would come to the *palapa* and give me moral support. El had been a nurse and was more knowledgeable about shots than I. El demonstrated, showing me how to be sure there was no air bubble in the syringe. She made me give the shot and it wasn't hard. Ink didn't mind at all. Besides, she was feeling better. I plied her with chicken noodle soup and scrambled eggs and she did eat a little. Each afternoon, I plugged her in the rear with another shot of penicillin. Think Ink realized the shots were helping. She'd look around at me as if to say, "Carry on nurse, go ahead and do it."

All the kids brought Ink flowers and patted her. I was touched by that. They knew how much I loved this animal and were concerned, not so much for Ink as for me since they recognized that she was more than just a dog to me. By Thursday morning when I took her temperature, it was normal. Called Wenseslau with the good news and breathed a sigh of relief. Never did find out what the infection was, but hoped that I hadn't exposed Ink to it by trying to help Sultan when he was so sick.

We finished the shots and Ink was slowly coming into her own again. Eating and tail wagging. I was having chili for dinner on Friday evening and she kept nudging me, so I gave her a bowl of chili. It was what she wanted and it worked miracles.

# # #

Re-joined the Christmas festivities now that my gal was mending. Charles and Mary Lou Stewart had a big dinner party on the 23rd. They butchered "Miss Piggy" and everyone brought a dish. Mary Lou was a wonderful cook, and we all savored "Miss Piggy" and the desserts that Mary Lou provided. I had found canned sweet potatoes at CCC and made orange cups with them topped with marshmallows. All had a great time, visiting and eating.

Got home in time to take Ink for a walk. Then, turned in early because the 24th was the Big Day. I had checked with the kids and they told me if they got any presents it was on the 24th before the family went to church. I suggested they come by the *palapa* between three and four. That was all the planning I did and I prayed fervently this would all work out.

Had just dozed off when out on the lawn there arouse such a clatter I sprang from *mi cama* to see what was the matter. Maestro, who lived two houses down the road on the other side of the street, was having a party. The whole barrio was vibrating. Ink muttered something about the damned loud music, but did not move from her pillow. I discovered that everyone in the Barrio was dancing to the great salsa music. I joined them since it was impossible to sleep. Never did crawl into bed until 2 a.m.

# # #

In spite of dancing the night away, by three the next afternoon the tree was lit and Santa was ready. There were thirty-one wrapped presents plus two pounds of M&Ms. I hoped it would be enough. Had decided not to have the children open their gifts in the *palapa*. Seemed too chaotic, since I had no idea of how this was going to work.

First to arrive was Jorgito and Lula — bright-eyed and shining. They each gave me a hug and away they went with their special gifts. Then, four of my little girls from up the hill. They, too, were just beautiful as everyone was ready for family fiesta and church. Mirna, Cariña, and Zulema along with Ramon slipped in. The girls had baked a white cake for me lettered in red with "Feliz Navidad, Barbla." It all flowed so well, this wonderful outpouring of love.

By four, most of the presents were gone. Then a group of boys I didn't know came to the door. One young lad really tugged at my heart. He was about six or seven and looked like a character straight from Dickens — a real scamp. He said, "My Dad's a policeman and he knows you. Do you have any cars?" I had one little car left in the basket and I knew this one needed it. Luckily, the other lads were older, so they got pencils and the scamp got the last car.

By 4:30 everything was gone including the two pounds of M&Ms — no one went away empty handed. I closed the door and had a quiet few minutes. My heart was full. My gift was all some of the kids would have. It was so good to know that I brought some joy and happiness to these lovely children. The true spirit of Christmas. It was more meaningful and satisfying to me than to them, I'm sure.

Ink and I took a long, sunset walk. She trotted along feeling much better. I had so much to be thankful and grateful for on this Christmas Eve.

# # #

Christmas day, I baked a pecan pie in the toaster oven, packed up Tessie, took my cake and drove out to Cerritos for another fiesta with the campers there. We had turkey, ham, and all the trimmings. A lovely group of people and very nice, but it didn't hold a candle to the celebration in Barrio San Ignacio.

Ink and I spent a few quiet days at the beach. She was well and loved romping with her dog friends. Adam came and changed oil and put the new filter in Tessie.

# # #

Got back to a very quiet palapa the 28th. The barrio was silent and it was golden. Had a hot tub, hopped into bed early, and was asleep immediately. The year was winding down and so was I. It had been a delightful season — one of good will toward men in a different culture and one in which I learned we truly are all family.

# # #

Hermalinda and Mirta invited me to the New Year's Eve dance. I declined since I didn't feel like wrestling around the plaza. Much as I love to dance, it didn't seem the night for me. Walked over and visited with Jorge and Elisa for a while, then settled down in my thatched roof home with Ink.

The end of 1989 was here. What an exhilarating year it had been. Thought back to New Year's Eve in 1988 when

Life in Barrio San Ignacio 155

Samantha, Theo, and I had dinner at El Patio in Mesilla. Had anyone said then that I'd be at home in a Barrio in Baja California, I would have never believed it. But here I was.

1988 was a wonderful year, once I got on the open road. And, 1989 was even more expanding — filled with learning and living in a different culture. Said a prayer of thanks to my gods and guides for still more joy in my travels and the blessings bestowed upon me. Snuggled into bed and said out loud, "Come on 1990!"

# # #

Early in January, Anita, the gallery owner in Cabo, called me and invited me to an opening for a Mexican painter named Pescina on the 19th. Decided I needed a break, so packed Tessie and Ink and drove South. A few spouts were visible on the Pacific. The whales were coming at last.

I pulled into our old haunt, Cabo Cielo, made arrangements for space, fixed dinner for Ink and me, took a walk around the grounds. Then we drove into Cabo for the opening.

Had an entertaining evening with Anita and her guests. She graciously invited Ink in from the camper. Ink preferred the canapes to the paintings. Anita's creative specialty was hand painted tiles. She showed me a large map of the Baja Peninsula done with her tiles. I liked a number of the paintings, mostly Baja and ocean scenes priced around $500 to $700, but found the Baja map tiles that Anita made my favorite.

We spoke of my neighbor Julian, who was a painter. He had a nice studio in Todos Santos and that's where he stayed. Anita told me she considered him very talented, but he would not promote his work. For that matter, the featured artist at the opening never did appear.

#

Spent a quiet night at Cabo Cielo. Had decided to do some exploring for a few days. Felt confident I could make my needs known in Spanish and understand what was being said to me. I had noticed on a detailed map a circle trip that looked inviting.

We left Cabo early and drove north on Route 1. Stopped for gas in San Jose, then on north looking for a sign leading inland to the town of Miraflores. I had read that it was a farming and cattle center, noted for fine leather work. From there, the map showed a road leading on to Santiago, the town with the only zoo in Baja. Thought this would be a nice dive, then planned to take another dirt road along the Gulf from La Ribera back inyo San Jose del Cabo. It all looked good on the map.

It was obvious that tourists did not often visit Miraflores. I stopped in the dusty, flower-laden village and was immediately surrounded by the citizens. Spoke with them and they assured me I was on the "road" that would bring us to Santiago with no *problemas*. The "road" was more a cattle path. We saw lots of cows, a lone *hombre* on a horse, but not one car. I had to keep going since there was no way to turn around. It was nice country and we enjoyed all the cows, but I wondered if we would ever reach Santiago. Ink was muttering something about, Oh, my God, we're hopelessly lost again. Just kept moving and eventually we came to Santiago. The road ran beside the zoo, so I took a quick turn. There was a bear, some monkeys, goats, and lots of birds.

In the center of town there were beautiful old churches and the Plaza was more impressive than the zoo. The wind was cool. I walked and took photos and thought it a paradise lost. Ate some lunch in the camper. Found a paved road that led us back to Route 1.

Life in Barrio San Ignacio

Drove into La Ribera on paved road, but that's where it ended. So we bounced along with the Gulf in view to our left, but could find no roads leading out to the sea. Just kept going — slowly. A blue VW camper with British Columbia plates passed me and I waved them down. They assured me there was great camping ahead. So we just kept going, and going, and going.

About the time I had decided it was all an illusion, we came round a bend and there was the bluest, loveliest bay and some campers. Pulled in and everyone waved. This looked good. Found a level spot and parked. Ink and I took a turn around this heavenly beach. There were lots and lots of dogs which pleased Ink. Everyone was friendly and welcomed us. Most of the campers were wind surfers from British Columbia. Those boards flitted around the bay looking like colorful butterflies. It was worth the long drive.

The wind was up and cold. The Canadians were in shorts and I was in sweats. Guess I had been in this tropical climate too long. Set up my chair on the leeward side of Tessie and while Ink played with the raft of dogs, I sat and watched wind surfers skitting across that incredibly blue bay. Everyone stopped to visit. Nice people and a nice spot.

Settled in early and slept well with the soft moaning of the Gulf punctuated by the gusty winds which rocked us to sleep.

# # #

Ian, a British Columbian, stopped and had coffee with us in the morning. He had been coming to this bay for 15 years. Did not do a lot of surfing now, but still enjoyed the area and the people. I asked him about the road on south. He assured me it was passable, just very rough. Enjoyed eating outside and watching all the activity, but pulled stakes and bounced on south along the Gulf.

Ian was right. The road was rough, so rough we were traveling 10 miles an hour. Lots of cattle, lots of erosion, lots of deserted blue lagoons. The scenery was spectacular, so slow going didn't matter. We stopped often just to feast on the vistas — and to rest my arms. A few miles south of Punta Arena, there was a monument sitting by the road. We got out and took a look. It was a stone marker mounted on a concrete pad overlooking a small cove with water so blue it looked purple. The marker stated this was where the Tropic of Cancer crossed the Baja.

Just below Cabo Pulmo, we spied a road leading down to another lavender lagoon. Pulled in and parked. Walked down to that lovely cove and waded for a while. Had some lunch, then back to bouncing.

About 3:30, both Ink and I had had enough driving. I decided we'd not make it into Cabo San Juan that day, so started looking for a spot to park for the night. We passed a converted bus with Utah plates parked off the road, so knew there were people about. A few miles further, saw a great level pad just off the road and knew it would be fine for a night. The land was level and accessible, then dropped down to a beach strewn with huge boulders. It looked perfect.

Set up quickly and Ink and I scrabbled down to the beach for a swim. The wind had died down and it was warmer here on this sheltered bay. The beach was smooth, but covered with spindle shells of all sizes. The boulders reminded me of Henry Moore sculpture. A great place to spend the night. Knew I might not have parked in such a desolate spot in some areas. Here on the Sea of Cortez, I felt safe and secure.

Fixed an early dinner, watched the sunset, and Ink and I snuggled in for a good night's sleep. Could see a faint glow in the night sky to the south. It made me think we could not be that far from Cabo. Perhaps we'd get there tomorrow if the road wasn't washed out.

# # #

The sun rose out of the azure Gulf like a large orange globe. It looked more like a sunset than a sunrise. There were a few cars on the road, moving slowly and quietly. The big Utah bus lumbered past. We had breakfast, then headed for the Henry Moore beach for a few more hours of swimming and checking out all the sculpture. I gathered more spindles.

About one, after a light lunch, we drove on south. It was just a short hop into San Jose del Cabo. In fact, the entire trek down the Gulf from La Ribera was only 50 miles. And it took us two glorious days to make the trip. The paved roads felt smooth as glass. Drove on to Cabo San Lucas. Made a quick stop at the *panadería,* then north. There were spouts all over the Pacific. The whales had arrived! It was early, so we headed down a familiar dirt road south of Cerritos. This one led to a high cliff with a great panoramic view of the sea and the south outcropping that we had hiked to. Parked and sat there looking at spouts everywhere.

Ink and I slid down the sandy bank and sat on the beach on a high hill overlooking the sea. It was here I learned that Ink was the best whale-spotter one could hope for. We were sitting side by side looking at the sea when Ink got quite nervous. Her nose was twitching and she was upset. Until that huge whale floated up out of the water right at our feet, I didn't know what was bothering her. I had never thought about the smell those beasts would have, and, for that matter, I couldn't smell anything. But Ink could detect them even before they surfaced. I could hear him. The Grey's song is not as melodious as the Humpback's — but they do sing. It was awesome.

Everyone told me the whales came into shore to rub barnacles off. This big, old guy rose to the surface, muttered a bit, then submerged and caught the tide. I calmed Ink and we sat close together and marveled over that whale right under our noses. He did his neat stunt three times in the same spot then disappeared into the depths.

Finally pulled away from the spectacle and got back to the *palapa*. All was quiet in the barrio. Unloaded, ate a little dinner, took a luxurious bubble bath and climbed into bed with visions of Grey whales dancing in my head.

# # #

Pam's packets arrived each month and were so welcomed. Pam kept the lines open, sending me statements and all relevant business items. It always took me a day to go over everything, but I rather liked that connection to the "other world." In the January packet, Pan reminded me that Ink needed her vaccines. Thank God, Pam kept me informed. Indeed, Ink had to have her shots.

Called Wenseslau and set up an appointment. It's a different procedure in the Baja than in the States. Rather than one shot to cover everything, he told me there would be a series of three shots at two week intervals. He explained that the vaccine is much more potent than what we need in the US. Therefore, Ink got hepatitis and lepto the first week, parvo on her second visit, and finally rabies. This is the order of most danger to the dogs here. So far, there were no heart worms in Baja. It meant three trips to La Paz to be sure Ink was protected and safe. After her bout with the infection, I would take no chances with my faithful companion.

# # #

We were making frequent runs to the north beach for

Life in Barrio San Ignacio

Moby-dicking. I couldn't get enough of those magnificent whales. Knew the smell bothered Ink, but she would sit next to me and let me know when one was close. In the large bay north of town, I counted 74 spouts in a half-hour one evening. Seemed the whales surfaced and played at sunrise and sunset. I tried to get some photos, but they didn't turn out. Amazing that a creature so large could be totally invisible just under the surface of the protective sea.

# # #

Mario decided that he was leaving for Mexicali. As he put it, there were no women here in Todos Santos. I was relieved he had accepted the fact that I was not interested in marrying him. With his decision, I gave Hermalinda the Christmas tree. Mario and Hermalinda had both asked for it. If Mario was leaving, he didn't need a tree. She planted it in the front yard at the corner of the house. Said she'd always remember me when she looked at the *arbolito*.

# # #

Sunday, February 11, Dale came to do her wash. Her machine was broken. I had finished breakfast and discovered my propane tank was empty. That meant no hot water and no means of cooking. Dale said she'd have it filled on Monday. I decided I'd be more comfortable in Tessie, so packed and drove out to the escarpment south of Cerritos for more Moby-dicking. Whales were everywhere.

Camped for three days marveling at those cetaceans. Each morning I'd sit outside and have coffee watching the whales cavorting in the Pacific. There's nothing to equal breakfast with the whales. Then, at sunset, they all came out to play again. I was royally entertained.

# # #

Our second morning, a VW camper pulled slowly into the area. As it passed, I could hear dogs barking. It went on by, then did another pass and stopped. I noticed the plates were from British Columbia. A good looking, tanned woman got out and walked over. Margaret was from Denman Island, BC. She had come to the Baja each winter for 11 years. A solitary woman with two dogs; a Dalmatian named Georgie Gal and a Heinz variety named Cody. All the dogs sniffed and decided to be friends. I asked Margaret to sit down. She decided we were good company and parked up a few yards from us. So I had company spying on the whales.

Woke early on the 13th wondering why that date was perking me. Dawned after the first cup of coffee. I had been in the Baja for one full year. Margaret and I toasted the occasion as we sat and watched whales. What more could one ask?

She, like all my friends in the States, asked how long I planned to stay. I smiled and told her I had no idea. But, I was beginning to think I should move on. Knew if I didn't pull myself away from this paradise soon, I'd never leave.

# # #

When we left for the *palapa,* I invited Margaret to come and visit. The two of us had had such an enjoyable time watching whales and visiting. She accepted and told me she would come and see that thatched roof *casa* of mine.

# # #

Margaret stopped at the palapa the 15th. Her Georgie was not well and she was concerned. I told her I had an excellent vet in La Paz. She said she spoke no Spanish. Ink still had one more shot to take. Wenseslau and I had been talking too much and he gave Ink the same vaccine twice. She still needed her rabies. I had an appointment on the 16th and suggested that Margaret meet us at the office and I'd try to interpret for her. She was very grateful and I was happy to do it. We had tea and Margaret left saying she'd see us in La Paz.

#

We were in Todos Santos the next day and Tessie developed a problem. When I started her, the charge light came one. I checked the belts, but they seemed okay. The light was still glowing and that disturbed me. Stopped at a friend's house and she suggested an electrical mechanic just down the street.

Tessie made it to Sergio's garage. He, as most Mexicans, was a born mechanic. Took a look under the hood and informed me the battery cables were filthy and she had two burnt out fuses. He fixed those in a few minutes, then adjusted the carburetor and Tess was purring. What a relief it was such a simple thing! I realized if Tessie ever needed a part of some kind, we'd be waiting for months to get it here in Todos Santos. The mechanics were so adept at improvising, I was sure we'd be able to keep Tess running. Adam had taken on steady work and was unable to give time to Tess's well-being any longer. I was delighted to discover Sergio.

#

Left for La Paz about 9:30 am and it was on the trip I noticed I was getting no reading on the gas or temperature gauges. Nothing serious, but it bothered me.

Got to the vet's a bit before eleven and Ink had her *vacuna*. Timing was perfect. Margaret walked in and I introduced her to Wenseslau, then proceeded to be an interpreter. Margaret would give me symptoms in English and I would tell Wenseslau in Spanish. It worked very well. He felt Georgie had a build-up of uremia from too much protein in her diet. He noted she also needed to lose some weight. Margaret liked this vet as much as I. We had a nice session in which he aired his views: too much protein in the dog food in the States, not enough exercise for the dogs or the people. He preferred to change diet before using any medication and fely two light meals a day were better than one.

Margaret asked if we could meet for lunch. I told her I'd meet her at the *malecon* in a few hours. There was a broad parking area and a nice view of the bay. Margaret suggested we just walk over to Harry's Place which was right on the Bay. We had a tasty lunch while watching boats on the Gulf.

She was now with friends in La Paz. Couldn't thank me enough for helping with Georgie. Said she'd be back in Todos Santos. I told her the welcome mat was always out at the *palapa*.

Got back to Todos Santos in time to stop and ask Sergio about the gauges. He raised the hood, adjusted something, and all was fixed.

# # #

The bridge had been devastated by Hurricane Kiko on August 27. By the middle of December, it was rebuilt. I found this a marvelous feat since the bridge was constructed with no heavy equipment. The Baja doesn't have road equipment as we know it. Most of the labor is by hand with shovels, pick-axes, and wheel barrows. But the bridge was rebuilt and operable. The workmen built a large concrete apron at the bottom and it all looked very solid. It certainly cut down on mileage into town. The road, at first, was muddy, but passable.

With some heavy rains in the mountains, the *presa* raged again and flooded the *huerta*. I was on my way to town, sailing down the road, over the bridge, and at the new apron I met a lake. Whoa! Was sitting there thinking it looked deep and forbidding when Señor Guillarte zipped by me in his Datsun pick-up, waving and saying come on. I patted Tessie and waded into the lake. It was deep, but

Life in Barrio San Ignacio

Tess kept cranking and we made it. Señor Guillarte was idling on the other side and threw me a kiss. The flood didn't subside for weeks, but after the first crossing, I just used the waterway to town.

# # #

Along with the whales, the cold winds also arrived. The days were sunny and brilliant, but the wind was chilling. With no windows, the gale was blowing me away. Seemed I was always grappling with frigid weather and I hate to be cold. Used some ingenuity and taped cardboard on the windows in the bathroom and the kitchen. It helped, but the *palapa* was a tomb when the sun went down. Slept in my sleeping bag and still shivered. Ink thought the weather was great. The fleas were not so vociferous and she appreciated the respite.

I had my quartz heater on the floor under the table and it kept my feet warm, but I was cold. Would join Elisa, Hermalinda, and Mirta each morning on the sunny side of the *palapa* for coffee, conversation, and warmth. It was always, *"¿Hace mucho frio, no?"* To which I'd nod and say, *"Si"* with my teeth chattering.

# # #

"La Gripe" blew in with the cold winds. Half the pueblo was wheezing and sneezing. The kids were coughing and running at the nose. Knew I couldn't escape this bug with all the kids in and out. And, I did get *"la gripe."* I swear, it was the most potent flu bug I've ever battled. Felt like a truck had run over me; my head throbbed, my throat was sore, I went through six boxes of Kleenex in a week.

Everyone in the barrio was feeling lousy, so I had lots of company for my misery. Elisa would just sit in the sun and sleep. I took my cues from her. Hermalinda brought me oregano tea. I was sleeping for ten hours each night and then taking a siesta. Had no energy whatsoever.

As with all things, *la gripe* passed, but it was a bug I could have done without. I would hear Jorge yelling at the kids when they tried to stop after school, *"No molesten a Barbla; está enferma."* He was so right.

Slowly gained strength and felt better, but paced myself since everyone did more than one round with this bug. The kids just kept going to school and running around spreading germs in their wake. There was no doctor in Todos Santos, but there was a clinic. I could have gotten a shot. After Wenseslau telling me how strong the vaccines for the dogs were, I was afraid the shots for the people were the same. Drank lots of oregano tea, lots of liquids, and slept lots of hours. *La Gripe* finally went away.

# # #

Mirna and Juanito's mother, Cariña's mother, and Zulima and Ramon's mother were all sisters. I would watch the kids carrying blue enameled kettles from house to house many evenings. The sisters often fed their families communally. Seemed a good idea. They combined forces and all ate at one or another of the houses.

# # #

The kids came in one morning and told me they were going to slaughter a pig. I was invited, but declined. Lupe's husband strung the pig in a tree by its hind legs and slit its throat.

I could hear that poor pig gurgling its last and dying. It disturbed me until I realized that 100 years ago in the States my relatives did the same thing. I strolled over once the pig was butchered. All the families were processing the meat. They ground most of it for *chorizos,* rendered some for fat and *chicharones.* I was lucky enough to have some *chicharones* — crisp and tasty with a good squeeze of lime from the tree nearby.

I asked Ramon if this had been one of his pigs. He said,

no, they were too young. Tweedle-Dee and Tweedle-Dum could still run around the neighborhood. In spite of the surprise they gave Ink and me standing in the yard, I was happy to hear we'd see them again.

# # #

Dale canceled Spanish classes since only Mary Lou and I were attending. She had decided to go into Real Estate full time and could not give four hours a week to Español. Mary Lou and I then met and studied together from time to time. Neither of us had trouble being understood, but we had trouble with some of the verb tenses. Spanish has 14 verb tenses and it's not an easy task sorting them out.

Loved talking with the Stewarts and listening to the birds on the veranda. Mary Lou always had something tasty cooking. Charles would show me his paintings. Since the Stewarts' was a meeting and greeting place, I touched base with many of the townspeople while there. Always enjoyed the visits even though I still had difficulty with Spanish verbs.

# # #

When I was in town one day, I stopped at the dentist, Antonio's, and asked if he could make a partial plate for one tooth I had lost while I was still in Las Cruces. I had had problems with the tooth for years. I grated on it while asleep.

In California, I had four dentists and one medical doctor working in my mouth. No one could understand how the tooth stayed in my jaw since I had no bone support to hold it. We were able to stabilize it and the tooth stayed put for 12 years. Then, it became infected and had to be pulled. My Las Cruces dentist wanted to do a permanent plate for the sum of $2400. I asked about a partial and it would have cost $1200.

So, I inquired if this lad could do a partial. Antonio said

he could. I stopped for an imprint, he checked the color of the enamel and told me it would be ready in eight days. The cost in Todos Santos was just a little less that $100. Antonio might not have had spiffy new equipment, but his price was right and the new tooth was perfect. I still use it. It's much better that a permanent tooth because I still grind my teeth from time to time.

# # #

With the new tooth, I decided I wanted my ears pierced, too. Mexican earrings were gorgeous, but made only for pierced ears. I asked Hermalinda and Mirta about getting it done and they offered to come with me to the clinic. Both patted my shoulder and told me, *"No se duele, Barbla."*

First order of business was a pair of gold earrings to wear while the holes were healing. I stopped at the *farmacia* and was entranced by the selection. Most of these gold ones were delicate and meant for the young babies since they had their ears pierced at a much younger age than I. Had trouble choosing . Finally bought one set of golden apples with a small bite out of the side, and another set of golden turtles, thinking, if you can't get mother turtle to hatch, wear the babies in your ears.

I was paying for them when the clerk asked if I wanted her to pierce my ears. It was free with my purchase of the earrings. I had a few misgivings, but knew this young lady was competent. Said, okay, and sat down in the small office. She used some antiseptic and a small punch and *"no le duele."* It was over in a minute, and Linda, the clerk, put the golden apples in my lobes. I was to turn them frequently and use some peroxide for sanitary cleaning. Got home and went over to show *mis vecinas* my new look. Elisa and Hermalinda approved. I was delighted in spite of being a bit older than the usual piercing recipient.

#

On my trips around the village, everyone waved and yelled, *"Hola, Barbla."* I was recognized. Enjoyed waving in return and had a few older residents that I looked forward to seeing. One, an old man, was always sitting on his porch. The other, a tiny, frail little *abuela,* lived in a tiny concrete house by the road. She was always dressed in black. Some mornings she would be rocking on her porch. Sometimes she would be tending her chickens, but we always waved.

As I was passing one morning, there were people standing around *abuela*'s house — kids, older people — a big crowd. I didn't stop but when I got home, went next door and asked what was going on. Elisa fixed coffee and told me that *abuela* was dying. Her family was there, grandchildren, friends, everyone who cared for her. All doing a vigil and offering support as she left this world. No sterile, white room in a hospital, just love and support for *abuela* as she died in her own home.

Next day, the crowd was still gathered. I knew she had not left us yet. The following morning, Elisa came over and told me, *"Abuela murió."* I was saddened by the death, but thought what a humane way to go — death with dignity and loved ones near.

#

March came in like a lamb. The weather was great, but the wind was chilly. I knew this would not last. The Pacific turns cold in March and the fogs roll in. The whales were swimming north and the tourists were going the same direction. Cerritos was deserted except for El and the dogs. I preferred it that way. El mentioned that she didn't welcome the cool foggy mornings of March and April. I felt the same way.

#

A small inner voice — my gypsy spirit — was beginning to whisper that, perhaps, we should follow the whales on north. I had mixed emotions about leaving this paradise, but was beginning to long for the open road and more travels. Did not push any decisions. Knew the way would become clear in good time.

# # #

With Pam's March packet, she enclosed a note reminding me that my driver's license would expire on the last day of April. I called and asked if she would find out how I could renew my New Mexico license from the Baja. The letter telling me how to go about a renewal *in absentia* was discouraging. I read all those formidable rules and regulations and knew the DMV would screw up for sure. Seemed wiser to get to New Mexico and acquire my license in person.

Along with the need for a new driver's license, my Mexican automobile insurance would expire on May first. If I was still in Todos Santos, I would have to get a new policy for an another full year. Asimex only wrote them that way.

The path was becoming clear. Gypsy spirit was showing the way. Knew, too, that I had to give Dale a month's notice since she had the last month's rent on deposit. This meant that I should come to a decision no later than March 15. I let it perk for a few days. Called Dale and informed her that I would vacate my beloved *palapa* April 15.

# # #

Had asked Dale not to say anything of my decision. Should have known the grape vine was alive and well. When I stopped at Stewart's, both Mary Lou and Charles knew and told me they'd miss me. It seemed to be common knowledge in the English speaking community, but was still unknown in the barrio. I hoped it would remain that way. Could not bear saying good-bye to all my neighbors for a full month.

# # #

Life continued its tranquil pace in Barrio San Ignacio. The roosters greeted the dawn, livestock noises drifted into the *palapa* as I sipped my morning coffee, the kids stopped each day, and neighbors were in and out. I viewed it all from a different perspective now that I knew I was leaving. Savored each moment. I had found this interlude so delightful.

Think we all would be better served if we looked at each day as if it were our last. For that matter, there are no assurances that it won't be. We spend too much energy and time fretting about what tomorrow will bring. Today is what we have — nothing more. Yesterday is gone, tomorrow has not come. Today is when we should live.

# # #

El and I had quiet lunches at the beach and the *palapa*. She planned to go to the States also. Offered an interesting proposition. "Why don't you move out to my trailer for a couple of months? If you wouldn't mind caring for the dogs and cats, the rent would be free." I had to think about that. Cerritos was very special and two months there was appealing. Told El I'd give her a decision in a few days.

# # #

The gypsy voice said, "No." It was time to leave. Much as I loved this place, I could not stay longer. El and I barnstormed my decision over lunch at Pilar's. "El, much as I'd like to stay longer, it's time to head north. First, I need a new driver's license and have until May 5 to get to Las Cruces. Second, my Mexican auto insurance expires May 1 and I need to be across the border or pay for another full year. Third, Ink tells me she cannot tolerate another summer of *pulgas* and hurricanes. And, fourth, that inner voice is saying it's time to move on. If I don't go soon, I'll never leave. I'll miss you, El, and I'll miss all my neighbors, but the time has come."

El understood and accepted my decision. It had been such a great experience living in the barrio and I had grown to love the people.

She smiled and said, "You know, your neighbors are going to be devastated when you tell them you're leaving? They love you, Barb, and they'll miss you. They'd give you the shirt off their backs."

"I know that, El, and I'm honored that these people have taken me into their hearts and been so kind. I'll miss the barrio and the beach more than you know. But I must follow that inner voice and get on with my journey."

# # #

Antonio called — my tooth was ready. It had been eight days right on the button. Drove into his office. *Abuelita*'s house was strangely quiet. When I arrived at Antonio's, he proudly displayed my partial and fit it for me. I felt like I had too many teeth. I had been a long time with that hole in my jaw. It did fit well. I could tell Antonio was pleased. We talked a bit and I smiled so he could admire his work. Paid him the last half of the charges for my tooth and thanked him for the good and prompt job.

# # #

Stopped at Stewart's. Jim was there looking crestfallen and sitting on the veranda. I asked if he were all right. He shook his head, no, and told me it was bad enough that I was leaving, but on top of that his truck was impounded by the police. Jim had never bothered with auto insurance. On his way to La Paz, he hit a horse and killed it. The police took the truck which was badly dented and impounded it until Jim paid for the horse. He had friends in La Paz who drove him back to Todos Santos, but was now walking and worrying. He had obtained a lawyer. He was fretting that the cost of the horse and repairs to his vehicle would be quite expensive. I offered to drive him around town. And, thought to myself, this is why I don't want to be without insurance in Mexico.

Jim was in better spirits by the time we got to his house. Invited me in for iced tea and I accepted. He kindly said that he would miss me. I told Jim how much I enjoyed our chats and that I would miss him, too.

# # #

Chuck and Julie, the young couple who had given the party at Loca Langosta, stopped to ask if I was really leaving. Seemed everyone knew of my decision. I explained that it was time. Was happy for the opportunity to ask some questions of Chuck — namely, if he knew of a good mechanic. Felt I should have Tessie check over and in shape for that long trip up the peninsula. Adam was working full time up the coast at Carozal and couldn't give Tessie his usual TLC. Chuck suggested Martin. Told me he'd be happy to take me to his garage and talk with him. Martin didn't much care to talk to women.

On the 8th of March, Chuck and Julie came by and led me to Martin's "garage." I would never have found the place by myself. We were on some roads I had never traveled. Bounced along in Tessie following Chuck and Julie. We finally came to a large, open field with a *palapa* sitting in the middle. There were cars and trucks scattered round the field and under the shade of the *palapa* a number of men working on vehicles. This was Martin's garage.

Chuck took the initiative and Martin talked to him. He slowly looked Tess over. Suggested a lube, draining and flushing the radiator, cleaning the carburetor, and checking all nuts and bolts. I understood all of this even though Martin was talking to Chuck about my machine.

He finally looked at me and asked, "It's okay?" I didn't want to upset this great mechanic, but had to ask about changing out the spark plugs. I thought it should be done before I left Todos Santos. Martin gave me a grudging smile and said, "Good idea." He then talked to me. Asked that I bring Tessie Wednesday morning, the 14th. She would be ready late Thursday. Chuck offered transportation to and from the "garage'.

# # #

Chuck and I were having iced tea at the *palapa* after leaving Tessie. All the children came to the window, as usual. The first question from Mirna was, "Where's the camper?" I told them I had to sell it so that I could buy more cookies for us. The kids knew I was teasing. We all laughed while I explained that Tessie was in the garage.

Chuck arrived early evening on Thursday and we went to pick up Tessie. The fellows were just finishing up. They had even armoralled the inside and offered to wash the outside. I told them that wasn't necessary. Martin spoke directly to me this time. He had given her a lube, cleaned the carburetor and adjusted it, changed spark plugs, drained and flushed the radiator, checked tire lugs, the battery water, and the belts. It was a thorough check. Martin insisted I start the camper. Tessie sounded brand new! For all this work, the bill was 75,000 pesos or less than #30.00 I thanked Martin and he wished me *un buen viaje*.

# # #

Felt Chuck and Julie had been so kind that I invited them to join me for dinner at El Molino on Saturday night. It was a nice evening. Great food and good conversation. All the patrons knew I was leaving and stopped at the table to wish me well.

# # #

I knew Tessie was ready for traveling, but realized how

much stuff I had accumulated and decided I must start weeding out. In spite of having too much stuff, I knew there were still a few acquisitions I had to take with me from this magic place.

Could not part with all the seashells, so packed them in boxes and put them in the storage bins below the seats. Had to have one of Anita's tile maps of the Baja, so drove to Cabo and visited her gallery. The timing was perfect. Anita was closing the big shop and moving to smaller quarters. She had one set of tiles left and sold them to me at a discount. While her helper was wrapping each tile separately and packing them in a box, Anita and I visited. She was staying in Cabo, but didn't plan to work as hard, so would only handle certain artists from her home. I thanked her for all her kindness. Told her I'd always remember her when I looked at the tiles. She asked when I thought I'd be settled. I had to admit I had not the foggiest idea.

# # #

Stopped at Cerritos with a birthday card and goodies from the *panadería* for El. She asked if I'd mind coming and caring for the livestock for a few days while she went over to the Gulf. Told her that would be good, since I wanted to wax Tessie and it was more fun at the beach. We agreed to split the time difference on our birthdays and have one celebration somewhere between the dates.

# # #

Drove out to Cerritos on the 17th. Pulled up in the corner inside the fence next to El's trailer. She had gone and only Madrita and a new female were there to greet us. There were just two rigs on the entire beach. I didn't socialize that evening. Walked with the dogs at sunset and turned in early. Sometime during the night, I woke and saw that Stud had come to join the caravan.

#

It would be my last time at this magical, mystical beach. I got Tessie waxed and sparkling and acquired more tan in the process. Alternated waxing work with walks and swims. Sat at sunset on my bluff overlooking the sea and pristine beach that was so special to me. It was more a temple of God than any church. I knew this spot was imprinted on my heart. I would never forget the joy and energy that flowed through me here at Cerritos. Said my good-byes with tears running down my cheeks. Thanked my gods and guides for leading me to this beach. Asked that they continue to lead me safely and well.

#

El returned on Monday, the 19th. Did not see her that evening, but she fixed pancakes and invited me for breakfast the following morning. We chatted about many things, but not my leaving. Neither of us wanted to say good-bye, but it was there. Finally, had to pull myself away and get on with sorting and packing at the *palapa*. El and I made a date to have our last supper at El Molino. I suggested Saturday, the 7th of April. Had decided to spend Easter week-end in the RV park there. Knew I could make arrangements when we had dinner.

Gave Madrita, Stud, Gilly, and the new female a hug and pat. Told El the new pup should be named "Feo" because she was really ugly. Hugged El and told her I'd see her the 7th. Then, drove slowly up the rutted dusty road with a heavy heart.

#

The 21st of March was a fiesta day — Benito Juarez' birthday. All the children were in and out. I looked at those darling faces and knew I'd miss them. Mirta and her family had completed their small concrete house down the hill from Jorge and Elisa. She sent Jorgito and Lula to invite me down to see the new *casita*. There were only two rooms. The main room contained two beds, a table, a two burner gas stove on the counter next to the sink, a cupboard, and three chairs. They had no electricity and no inside plumbing, but Mirta and her husband were gracious and warm. I had a glass of tea and a nice visit. Mirta was pleased that I had come. Still had not told anyone in the Barrio I was leaving.

# # #

In the midst of sorting and making decisions, I heard an unfamiliar male voice calling out one afternoon. Opened the door to a young man from the States. I had seen him around town and on the beach. Mike walked up to tell me that he had rented a *casa* down the hill from me. He was quite friendly and effusive. Said he was so glad that I was near and hoped we could be friends. I thanked him for stopping, but did not say I would visit him nor did I offer any help. My first thought was, "My God, the gringos are closing in on me." Somehow, this overly-friendly fellow did not ring true. Couldn't put my finger on what it was about his manner that bothered me, but he did not seem on the up and up. He left shortly and I went back to decision making.

# # #

The following Saturday night, I was reading in bed when I heard foot-steps hurrying around the portal. There was a knock on the door and a female voice asking, "Barb, are you there?"

"Yes. Who is it?"

"Barb, it's Nellie."

I yelled I'd be right there and jumped out of bed. Opened the door to Nellie and her daughter. Nellie was pale and upset. Got the two of them into the *palapa* and put the kettle on.

"My God, Nellie, what are you doing here?"

Then the story came out. My new, friendly neighbor had invited Nellie and Beverly Ann for dinner. When they arrived, he was rather drunk and there was no dinner in sight. Nellie told me she began to think she had made a poor decision, but had no car and no means of getting home. Mike kept drinking in spite of Nellie's request that he drive her to Pescadero. He fixed another drink and told her if she wanted dinner, she'd have to fix it. Finally, Mike suggested that she and daughter stay all night since he would not drive them home. He passed out and Nellie, being the survivor she was, remembered that I was up the hill. She wrapped Beverly Ann in a blanket and hiked up to the *palapa*. I fixed hot tea and we talked a while. Told Nellie not to fear, I'd drive her to Pescadero. Got into a pair of sweats and pulled out of the drive at 10:30.

On the trip, Nellie regained her composure and with it a healthy dose of anger. She used some choice epitaphs for that fellow I intuitively had not trusted. She stated that no Mexican lad had ever treated her that way. She thought she's just date only young natives who were courteous and honorable. Indeed, Nellie with her vivid green eyes and lovely fair skin, had more suitors than she could manage. I encouraged that thinking. Got to Pescadero and made sure Nellie and Beverly Ann were safely in the house, then drove slowly back to Barrio San Ignacio. It was a late night for me, but I was glad that Nellie had hiked up the hill. When I pulled into the drive, Salchicha, Petufo, and Indio were all sitting waiting for us. Don't know if Ink told them of our rescue of a damsel in distress or not.

# # #

Next morning, Elisa came over to invite me for coffee. She really wanted to know where I had gone in the middle of the night. Jorge was working on the old, blue Ford pickup. I sat and told them the whole story in Spanish. They laughed and agreed that you just couldn't trust those gringos.

#

The first of April, I told Elisa, Jorge, and the girls I was leaving. The dam broke. Seemed the grapevine in the Barrio was more efficient than with the gringo community. The kids started filing into the *palapa*. They were solemn and subdued. All asked if it was true that I was leaving. I nodded yes and explained that I had to go back to the States; that I wanted to see *mis hijos*. It was sad, but the children understood my decision. They all asked that *"Nunca olvídanos."* I hugged those darling kids and assured them I would never forget them or my life in the barrio.

#

Jorgito and Lula stopped to ask me down to their *casita*. They told me Mirta, their mother, was making *empanadas* and wanted me to have some.

Headed down the hill that cold, gloomy morning feeling like the weather. Mirta did not say much about my leaving. She demonstrated how she did her *empanadas* and asked if I cared to buy some. I loved this resourceful woman's ability to raise money. Told her I'd like three. She said Jorgito would deliver them.

Had just finished the empanadas when Scot called to wish me a happy birthday. We had a great visit and I told him I'd be leaving Todos Santos the middle of the month. Hoped to see both Scot and Mark in Phoenix in early May if we could put it together. The talk made me feel better.

Weather was typical for April: cold, foggy, and gloomy. I hopped into bed to stay warm. The barrio was very still that Sunday evening.

#

Monday, Mark and Lois called. Told them I was thinking

of continuing this journey and seeing the Pacific northwest and other areas in the West I had never visited. Knew if I didn't do it now, I'd never do it. As usual, the kids said, "Go for it, Mom. We'll meet you in Seattle." Told Mark of Scot's hope that we could all touch base in Phoenix and asked that the boys handle that while I negotiated the Transpeninsular. Thoughts of seeing my sons eased the pain of leaving Barrio San Ignacio.

# # #

Had a quiet birthday. Drove up to Carizal hoping to find Adam and Suzie, but no luck. Drove around the new farming community being developed there. Baja had discovered there was a market for produce in the States and was developing farms using underground water. Change was coming to *"la frontera."* Thanked my guides that I had been here before the great change took place.

Sat in the gazebo, watched another sunset, and contemplated my time in the Baja. The Barrio was good for me. I had learned so much from these people and had mellowed. Worried that the States and its cultural norms would throw me after this slow, *mañana* pace. Promised myself that I would strive to live only this day, to accept and not judge anyone, and to love. Recalled a passage in one of the many books I had read: The more you embrace and enjoy and accept, the more you are embraced and enjoyed and accepted. It surely was true of Barrio San Ignacio.

# # #

Thank God life went on as usual. Perla, the other female dog, came into heat. Ramon staked her out on the roof again. All the males congregated and fought and howled all night. Tweedle-dee and Tweedle-dum, the pigs, were in the yard one morning. Roosters still greeted the dawn raucously. The kids were at the windows each morning asking to come inside. The hectic routine continued in the barrio. Still found my sense of humor the best asset for dealing with all the chaos.

# # #

Now that everyone knew I was going, the ladies came to sit almost every evening. It was touching. They all told me they'd miss me and I reciprocated. I would miss them, but would also appreciate some privacy. I felt like I was attending my own wake.

Hermalinda told me I was the nicest gringa ever to live in the *palapa*. She hoped I would return for her wedding in December. This young woman had become near and dear to me. We could talk and laugh and did enjoy each other's company. Mirta told me that Jorgito kept saying I wouldn't go. I heard that Maestro told everyone the barrio would never be the same when Barbla left.

# # #

Jim was still without his truck. It was impounded and no one seemed inclined to resolve the matter. I drove him into town often and hoped someone else would come to his rescue after I left. Told him I had taken his good advice and would stay at El Molino until after Semana Santa and the surge for the beaches that it brought.

# # #

Mario was the invisible man. Stayed in his small concrete house and would not speak to me. In my last week, he stopped and we had tea. I thanked him for all his kindness and wished him well.

The children were wandering in and out, bringing me mementos — pictures, little scraps of paper with nice messages, and flowers. It was a draining time. I was glad I had not told anyone I was leaving sooner.

# # #

I knew I could not pack all the many things I had

accumulated. Gave Mirta blue enamel pots and pans I had bought in Todos Santos. She took the netting for Lula's bed and we all heaved *mi caballo* down the hill for my Jorgito. Elisa was always cold and I left her a pair of woolen socks I loved and a warm wind-breaker. For Hermalinda, two necklaces she had always admired. Weeded out clothing and gave a big bag to the poorest children in the Barrio. The girls could wear my clothes. Cariña took the National Geographic about China; Mirna choose the one with Indians. I doled out the rest of the magazines to some of the others. Jorge was delighted with my gift to him: two screw drivers, battery water, a short hose, cheese cloth, and the old vacuum that had been in Tessie since I bought her. Jorge told me he'd hang the screw drivers on the wall and think of me when he used them. This buddha of a man who had frightened me so much when I moved in had become a great friend. I adored him and it seemed to be mutual.

That evening, Ink was on the bed with me. I patted my gal and told her I thought we had better get away before I gave her and Tessie to one of the neighbors.

# # #

Margaret, my Denman Island friend, called from La Paz to let me know she was heading home. She thanked me again for the help with her dog at my vet. I told her of my plans to head north. Margaret invited me to come and stay with her, if I made it to British Columbia. I accepted with pleasure and said I hoped to see her again. We wished each other safe travels.

# # #

El and I had our last supper at El Molino on Saturday, the 7th. The weather was cool, but not as nasty as it had been the previous year. We ate and reminisced. So many things we had shared — the turtle eggs, trips to Cabo and

San Jose looking for insurance agents, spaying Madrita, so many shared experiences. We agreed that no matter where we went or what we did, we'd always be friends. It was a bittersweet meal since we knew I was leaving, but it was good to have one final loving talk with this good friend. El asked why I didn't come out to Cerritos after I left the *palapa*. I told her I couldn't stand one more good-bye. Knew it would be better to rest at El Molino for a few days after all the wrenching farewells in the barrio.

# # #

The tenth I did my last round of Todos Santos. Stopped at the *farmacia* and bought five pens. Three went to the fellows at the bank; one to my butcher at Guillarte's who kept my knives honed to a fine edge, and one to Antonio, the postman. Had one more acquisition to make. Stopped at Julian's studio and told him I had to have one of his paintings to remind me of this beautiful place. Julian allowed me to browse. I would have taken one of everything, but could not afford it. Finally had the choice down to two lovely scenes. One was a sepia of the roadway through the *huerta* lined with the huge eucalyptus trees, the other was a water color of the north out-cropping at Cerritos. Loved them both, but opted for the beach scene. Julian told me he would pack the painting well for travel and bring it by the *palapa*.

# # #

Hermalinda and Mirta said they'd love to go to the beach one last time before I left. We loaded Ink, Jorgito, and Lula into Tessie and drove north. The girls had packed a tape deck and some water. We stretched out in the sun and talked. Jorgito and Lula danced and played with Ink. Hermalinda and Mirta told me how very much they would miss me. I assured them I'd miss them, too. They had become good friends. I told them my time in Baja was one of the happiest experiences of my life.

# # #

On the 11th I popped the top on Tess and started loading. Told her the days of being a "town car" were numbered. Wound up the old GE and did bedding and rugs. Julian stopped with my painting well-wrapped for travel. And, of course, kids were everywhere. Got some of them organized to carry out stuff for packing in Tessie.

Later in the afternoon, the kids all serenaded me while we had our last round of cookies and juice in the gazebo. Got them away and was fixing dinner. Cariña and Mirna arrived for some last words. Mirna brought me photos of the family. Cariña wanted to know who I would miss the most. Really couldn't answer that. All the kids had entwined themselves around my heart. Shooed my two girls out and closed the door wondering if I could hold myself together for three more days. Then it was Hermalinda, Mirta, and Carmela for another round. This good-bying was draining me.

# # #

Kept the shutters and door closed in spite of kids on the portal begging to come in for another round of good-byes. Was fairly well packed and the *palapa* no longer looked like home.

Salchicha, Petufo, and Indio joined us for our last walk. There were lots of people on the *ejido* land. Families coming from La Paz to celebrate Easter in Todos Santos. Gave all the dogs dinner. Then, Ink and I went out to sleep in Tessie. As I was climbing in, I heard Elisa ask, *"¿Barbla, yendo?"*

I yelled, *"No, solamente durmiendo."*

Then, Jorge started with *"Mi querida, no te vas, mi amor, no te vas."* I started to laugh and told him he sounded like Mario. We all said, *"Buenas noches"* and Ink and I settled into our little womb.

# # #

Woke early. The barrio was strangely silent. Had some coffee, then lit the refrigerator in Tessie. Had some chores to finish in the *palapa*. Certainly did not look like home anymore. I defrosted the fridge, folded all the rugs and table cloths that I had laundered, swept well and did a little mopping.

Was beginning to think that I would escape without any more heart-breaking good-byes when Mirna, Juanito, Marlene, and their dog Indio stopped. They had more pictures and a note they had written saying they would always remember me. Hugged each of them and tears welled in my eyes. Mirna, who had been so special, was crying openly. Not an easy chore this leaving loved ones.

Kept plugging away. Put the last things for Mirta on Elisa and Jorge's porch. No one there. I breathed a sigh of relief. Had everything packed and was ready to pull out when Hermalinda, Carmela, her husband, Jorgito, and Lula pulled in next door. This had to be the final round. This family had been so kind and good to me. I knew I'd miss them and they told me they'd never forget me. I promised Hermalinda, when I got settled I would send an address and she said she'd write. Jorgito didn't say a word; just stood there with tears running down his cheeks. Hugged him and then I started sobbing. Retreated to Tessie and backed out of the drive. We all waved and sobbed as I blew a final kiss and headed down the road.

Crossed the bridge, drove among the eucalyptus trees, up the hill, and into town for the last time. Stopped at Guillarte's for quinine and cigarettes. Said a final *adios* to Señor Guillarte. Then out to the produce stand for the last strawberries and some produce. Got to El Molino about 3:30 totally worn out. We parked and popped up in a shady spot. When I hooked up, found the electrical system was A-ok.

Went for a long, hot shower. Ink and I took our siesta in Tess. She was snug and soothing. Knew the worst was over and felt excited about getting on the open road again. Yet, knew I would never forget my life here in Todos Santos.

That evening, I walked over to the restaurant and treated myself to dinner. Margarita, the owner and cook, hovered over me as always, anticipating my every need. The air was cool and the food was excellent. Took Ink for a short turn, then into bed.

# # #

Easter Sunday was quiet in the campground. I planned an easy day of getting myself together after all the farewells. Found it restful to sit and have coffee without any children calling through the windows. Ink and I strolled the grounds. Thought I'd just read and relax, but it was not to be.

Mary Lou stopped to wish me safe travels. She needed an address for the IRS and asked if I had one. Dug into my briefcase and got her an address. She grinned and said she was going to miss me. Settled back for more reading when Chuck and Julie arrived. Then, it was some people I had met at Cerritos. Dale, too, came by. She had been to the *palapa* and stopped to thank me for leaving it in such good shape. I thanked Dale for all the kindness. Told her she was one super landlady. We agreed when I was ready to return, the *palapa* would be available. Thought surely that was it when El and a friend stopped. These farewells weren't as hard as the barrio, but I still felt saddened by them. Finally, at dusk, we were alone. Ink and I had dinner and a stroll and went to bed early.

# # #

Decided on Monday to drive over to La Paz and avoid

any more visitors. Got away about 4 p.m. Stopped for one last check at the Post Office. Thanked Antonio for the good service. He told me he hoped I'd return and I said, *"Yo, también."* Was spending the night at El Cardon, an old park close to CCC. So it was an easy drive. One I knew well.

# # #

North on the Transpeninsular

Got into La Paz about six. It was hot and sultry. The old campground looked inviting. El Cardon was almost downtown and was an oasis in the middle of all the traffic and hustle bustle of the city. The spaces were ringed with bougainvillea and palm trees. It was well-run and clean.

Not too many tourists as we drove up the lane to our space. I was glad. Didn't feel the need for any socializing at all. I was wrung out from all the farewells. Needed some quiet time. Fixed dinner for Ink and me. Took a quiet stroll around the park and called it a night. Had the radio plugged in and my beloved La Paz station was playing loud and clear. Knew this would be the last time I could listen to the station that had been such a help with Spanish, so enjoyed it doubly.

#

Tuesday morning, there was a cool breeze and it was unusual not to have roosters or children pounding on my eardrums. Sat and drank coffee and enjoyed the quietness. Went up and had a shower, then walked Ink. Met three people from San Diego who were stranded in the park. A *Federales* car had plowed into one of their campers. They were all living in the other rig, waiting for repairs. Their story reminded me of a habit the drivers here in Baja have, which can be hazardous. If the highway is clear, the Mexicans turn on the left turn signal, meaning it's safe to pass. These Americans had turned on the left signal because they planned to turn left. The *Federales* car plowed

North on the Transpeninsular

right into them, because he understood the signal to mean it was clear to pass. I learned to turn left with my arm hanging out the window. It was much safer.

# # #

Pulled out of El Cardon early and drove down the street for my last marketing at CCC. Loaded up on supplies and bought a cassette with my favorite song, *"La Negra Tomasa,"* on it. Didn't want to get away from that great music too quickly. Left La Paz about ten, April 17, heading north.

Just a few miles out of town there was an inspection station. They were checking fruits and vegetables, but when the inspector saw Ink, he informed me that I needed a certificate for her. It cost 10,000 pesos. It was no problem, but I wondered if anyone would ever ask to see that certificate.

It was hot, but bearable along the coast. Clear highways and good music. It cooled as we climbed onto the Magdalena Plain. Pulled off the road south of Ciudad Constitucion, had lunch and a short walk, then across the Plain through Villa Insurgentes. More high open country until we reached the Sierra de la Giganta. Put Tess into second and we descended that tremendous chain of mountains — spectacular canyons and rugged scenery. Broke out on the Gulf side and started looking for the small sign for Juncalito. Pulled into that south sea setting about 4 p.m. and parked under the palms.

The *basura* from Semana Santa was stacked up just as Jim had warned me. We were back from the beach, so escaped the flies and dogs gorging themselves on all the garbage. Got set up and about that time Jose Maria, the caretaker, arrived. He was surprised by my command of Spanish. We had quite a chat. Jose Maria informed me that he worked each day from 10 until 6, but I noticed that he was just sitting amongst the litter doing nothing. He bummed two aspirins and a cigarette, then said it was time for him to go home. He did no litter removal at all.

There were a few campers, but no one near us. Decided in spite of the heap of *basura,* we'd stay here on this lovely beach for a few days. Had a nice sunset walk, then into bed with lots of birds muttering in the palms. It was much more quiet than the barrio.

# # #

Had a laid-back day at Juncalito. Jose Maria never did show for work that Wednesday. Ink and I hiked up the beach to a sandy cove and had a swim. There was a lot of seaweed along with the trash, but the water was calm and warm. Straightened the camper and stretched out for a bit of uninterrupted reading. Ink was under the camper in a hole she had dug.

I dozed off, but woke when I heard Ink giving her greeting cry. Someone was asking, "Is that you,Ink?" Ink was doing her best to say indeed it was. Looked out and there were Jack and Nadine, the wonderful California couple who had been at Cerritos with us in '89. It was old home week. They were staying in Loretto and insisted that we stop for a visit before heading on up the peninsula. Jack and Nadine were going south with a new Dodge Diesel pulling their 5th wheel. I told them we'd come into Loretto on Thursday and fill them in on my glorious year.

# # #

Thursday morning, we strolled the littered beach. Ink romped with the scavenging dogs. I swam and picked up more shells. Did some bird watching and was able to identify a Phainopipla. When a pick-up carrying 16 people pulled into the beach, Ink and I closed camp and headed for Loretto.

The drive was as beautiful as I remembered with the Gulf

on one side and the Sierra de la Gigantas on the other. The road was as horrid as when we drove down, but by this time I was used to Baja roads and just bounced along. Didn't even attempt to miss the numerous potholes.

Las Palmas was crowded with a group of Californians. We drove over to the other campground and located Jack and Nadine. Bud, the owner, was from the States and a delightful host. He was laid-back and had a herd of dogs of all sizes and descriptions. He offered to take Ink, but I said no way. The facilities were good, in spite of no shade. We parked up near Jack and Nadine.

The kids here were constantly begging. Decided there's a direct correlation between the begging and how many tourists visit an area. Never had a child in Todos Santos begged. They were much too proud for that. I dispatched the kids with. *"No me pidan nada."* Knowing the language certainly helps.

The fishermen were putting in and I walked down to view the catch. Asked for a small sierra. Cleaned it and put it into the toaster oven with a dab of butter and a squeeze of lime. Went for a much-needed shower. The sierra was baked when I got back. After dinner, Jack, Nadine, and I sat and visited while the shadows deepened on the Gulf islands.

# # #

Friday I stayed at Bud's. Jack and Nadine took me into town to tour the large, new super market. I stocked more supplies. Got to the bank, then had lunch at Playa Blanca while we filled each other in on what we had done for the past year.

Were back to the park in time for a siesta. Ink and I took a walk on the rocky beach. Went over and showed Jack and Nadine photos of the *palapa* and Todos Santos. Had an early dinner and into bed with sounds of music playing, dogs barking, people laughing. Rolled over and knew I was going to miss this.

#

Saturday, much as I loved the company, decided I should wander on north. Did a load of laundry before breakfast, visited more with Jack and Nadine. Told them I planned to do the final western loop before I gave up my life on the road. They insisted I call them, if I got to their area in Northern California. I promised I'd check in if I was still going by then.

Jack suggested I stop at San Lucas for the night. Still on the Gulf side and he was sure I'd like the setting. Once again, fond good-byes and wishes for safe traveling. Pulled out of Loretto around three. Detoured again through Nopolo to rest my arms and give Ink a run. Nothing had changed and there were still no people at this fabulous resort the Mexican government was trying to develop. Thought of stopping in Mulege, but decided I had seen it and drove on to San Lucas.

The park was bare bones, but the Mexican owner was gracious and kind. He was delighted that I spoke Spanish. Told me he had a cousin in Todos Santos. We registered and pulled down to the bay. Ink was in the water immediately. It was filthy camper time again. She did carry in lots of sand and mud, but it was a small price to pay for her good company. Had dinner and turned in early. The water lapping on the shore was soothing. I had left the door open as it was warm. Could hear the ducks calling out on the islands. The cantina was crowded and there was guitar music and singing. Price for my spot here in San Lucas was $5.00.

#

Sunday morning was overcast. I sipped my coffee and watched fish jumping in the bay. Understood why so many fishermen liked Jose's camp. Walked Ink and had breakfast. Jose strolled over and invited me to stay a few days. He even offered to lower the fee from $5.00 to $3.00, if I'd spend more time. I thanked him and said, *"Yo tengo que ir a Estados Unidos y necesito llegar antes del primero de mayo."* He asked why I had to be back by the first of May. I told him my Mexican insurance ran out then.

He smiled and replied, *"Entiendo, pero venga otra vez."* I told him I'd return and stay longer. Went over and had a hot shower. The restrooms were not very clean, but the water was hot.

It was a short hop into Santa Rosalia. Pulled in for gas and found *no hay* extra. Asked if there was extra in San Ignacio and the lad smiled and said *"Sí."*

Just after Santa Rosalia, we turned inland and began the ascent up Sierra de Santa Lucia. I remembered that this was one horrendous drop, but heading south I was on the inside lane hugging the mountain on this narrow road. I also had views of the Gulf. Driving up that treacherous mountain was another matter. The road was narrow and curvy, two lanes, and no shoulders at all. There were no guard-rails and the drop-off was about 500 feet. I stole a glimpse over the precipice and wished I hadn't. There were rusting hulks of cars and trucks scattered down the mountainside. Said a silent prayer, gripped the wheel tightly, shifted into second, hoped a *camión* did not come careening down the mountain out of control, and kept laboring up the steep and narrow path. After what seemed an eternity, we reached the top. There was a broad berm here. I pulled off the road, took a deep breath, and thanked my gods and guides from the bottom of my heart for getting us safely up that mountain. Gave Tessie a pat for not missing a beat.

Got to San Ignacio about noon. The Pemex station on the highway was closed, so tried the station at La Pinta. *No hay* extra. Three fellows from California told me the regular wouldn't hurt Tessie. I figured my mileage and decided I could make it to Vizcaino. Was about to pull out of the station when a couple I had met and talked with at Juncalito were stopping at La Pinta for lunch. John told me to go ahead. They'd be behind and if I ran out of gas, they'd help.

So off we went thinking how typical of Mexico. Each town assuring you the next town will have gasoline and the next town assuring you the next town will have gas. No one wants to be discourteous.

Got to Vizcaino and *no hay* extra, of course. Gritted my teeth and had 20 liters of regular put in the tank. Then I got out and added a can of *aditivo*. The fellows assured me Guerrero Negro would have extra. I smiled and left. The weather was changing — winds up and scudding clouds. Tessie was running better on the regular than the extra so no problem reaching Guerrero Negro before 5 p.m.

Drove downtown and knew I had missed nothing on the southern trip by not visiting it. Not a very picturesque town; however, they had extra! Gave Tessie a long, cool drink. Dashed into the *panadería,* then pulled into the *parador* along the highway where we had stayed before. A new couple were behind the counter. I was sorry El Señor was no longer there. We could have had a really long talk in español.

Settled Ink and hiked over to the barracks for a hot shower. Stood there under the spray thinking, "It's a sure sign one is getting old when a hot shower fulfills sensuous pleasures." Tessie was warm and snug even though the wind was howling. Ink and I cuddled up and slept well. Grateful for gasoline and a safe, but scary, climb up Sierra

North on the Transpeninsular

de Santa Lucia.

#

Monday morning was cold and windy in Guerrero Negro. It was a three cups of coffee morning. Got dressed in warm clothes and Ink and I took a run around the park. Dogs came to play and I let Ink have some fun. We were on the Transpeninsular before ten. I could see no reason for sitting in that windy campground.

The wind was strong, but there was no traffic and we purred along. Turned into Santa Ines and had a delicious enchilada platter. Ink roamed around. No one minded my black dog who seemed able to converse with the Ranch dogs. After all, Ink was bi-lingual, too.

Then, it was the land of boulders and boojums. We enjoyed the striking scenery. Came out on the Pacific at El Rosario. A few miles north, I saw a sign for El Socorro RV park and turned down a rutted lane. The park did not look inviting so we parked south of it on the mesa.

We were high above the Pacific here. It was nice to see that broad sweep of ocean. I knew this would be the last time I'd be camping by the Pacific. Ink and I slid down the hill and walked the rocky beach. Had dinner, built a fire, and drank my last cup of Lapsang Souchong. Sam had kept me supplied with my favorite tea while I was in Todos Santos. Sipped tea, said *adios* with some regrets to the Pacific. Looked ahead to seeing friends in Las Cruces. Thought, here's to you, Sam. Be seeing you soon.

#

Tuesday, we got gasoline in San Quintin. We had plenty of time to make it to the border so I decided we should take a side trip to San Felipe. Negotiated Ensenada's wild traffic, but never did find Route 3 for San Felipe. We were north of Ensenada when I spotted Route 3 going north to Tecate. We took it instead.

Drove though lush countryside. There were boulders dotting the fields and mountains, fertile valleys with olive groves and vineyards. The large *ranchos* were well kept. I saw one campground, but it didn't look right, so kept driving. Never saw another RV park.

We were approaching Tecate and I knew I didn't want to tackle the border crossing that evening. Was wondering if Tecate had any camping facilities when off to my left I saw a sign reading: Tecate Country Club and Estates. In we went. Down a landscaped lane lined with eucalyptus trees. Came to a golf course with club house, tennis courts, and a pool. Then past an Inn and up the drive to an ornate hotel. I began to suspect this was nothing but a mirage. Parked at the hotel and went inside. It was fabulous, but there were no guests. A lone gal at the desk told me I could park under the trees down by the Inn.

We pulled onto a flat spot under eucalyptus trees and settled, then walked the grounds. Ink loved the golf course — rolled and enjoyed the first green grass she had seen in a long time. Just up from where we were parked was a small chapel. The grounds were neatly kept. Street lights lined the roadways and there was light in the chapel, but no people, not a soul in sight. It was eerie.

Found a water faucet close to our parking site and filled some bottles. Then climbed into Tessie for dinner and a bucket bath.

It was cool this far north. Got into bed and read for a while. Ink was snoozing. There were a few mutterings of birds in the trees, but nothing else. It was very still and very deserted here at Tecate Country Club and Estates. Felt like we were parked in the Twilight Zone. I hoped the spirits were friendly.

# # #

Next morning, I was so happy to hear voices. On our

walk, the mystery of the "mirage" was solved. Met the construction boss of this project. He was from the States. Told me the enterprise was owned by a wealthy Mexican who had 4,000 acres which he hoped to develop. I asked if there were brochures available, but there was no printed matter yet. Felt no one would believe my description of this place and had no film in the camera to prove it did exist. At least, I knew it was not all a dream. Thank God for my talk with the foreman.

We drove out the lane and onto the highway into town. Tecate is not a typical border town. Noted for its *cerveza,* the area was teaming with Tecate trucks. Did a turn around the plaza, went into the bank and changed pesos to dollars. It was only three blocks to the border. But, I spied Route 2 going east to Mexicali and decided I had lots of time, so took it. Seemed I was not anxious to get back to the States.

Route 2 was good highway, but we had one more mountain chain to hurdle. It was up and up and up. Topography was similar to that in California west of El Centro. Finally topped out on the mountain and then it was straight down to the desert. I was happy for small Tessie. Surely would hate to have a trailer behind me on that twisty downhill drive. Winds were up and sand was blowing across the desert. Luckily, Mexicali had a bi-pass and we avoided that large, industrial city.

We stopped at San Luis and ate in a restaurant. Told Ink this would be her last dining-out excursion. Then back to desert country on Route 2 to Sonoita. We were traveling in circles. This had been the road we took from Lukeville when we went to California. Knew the crossing at Lukeville was uncrowded and easy. It seemed the place to enter the States.

We pulled into the Border crossing about 4 p.m. I knew I could have told the guards we were coming from Puerto

Peñasco, but I was curious about how they would handle a gringa who had been in Mexico almost 15 months. When I answered the question on how long I had been in Mexico, the guard did a double take. He directed me to a parking bay. Another border official came out and asked to see inside the camper. I got out and opened the door. He just stood there looking at Ink wagging inside.

Without getting into Tessie, he asked me if I had any fruits and vegetables. I told him I still had some zucchini, guayavas, and limes in the fridge. The next question threw me. "Do you have any Irish potatoes?" I told him I did not. He then inquired why I had chosen to cross the border here. I explained I had been through this crossing before. Knew I could call from the phone booths and re-instate my USAA auto insurance. Planned to spend the night at Gringo Gulch on the other side of the chain link fence. That seemed to satisfy him and he waved me through. Still wonder about the Irish potatoes.

We had lots of room in the park. Spaces were now $12.50 and I gulped. No more $5.00 parking for us. We were in the United States.

Back Home Once More

The grounds were filled with birds and cool and crisp in the morning. Drank my coffee, then went for a shower and shampoo. The restrooms seemed very spacious after some of the Baja accommodations. Ink had to be on lead and chafed about that. We walked over to the phone and reinstated insurance on Tessie. Went across the arroyo and Ink had a good run.

Decided to rest for a day in this pleasant setting. I was weary from the long trek up the peninsula. Always told everyone the Baja drive separated the women from the girls. And, indeed, it was a strenuous journey. So we sat in the park and visited with the few people and relaxed. I was feeling sad and missing my barrio, my children, and my neighbors. I was between two cultures. Knew it would take time to get back into the swing of the States.

# # #

Friday I decided to drive to Tucson by way of Kitt Peak and the Papago reservation. Got away about ten. It was already hot in the sun. Ink was panting and scratching. She was suffering from this dry climate and her skin was flaking, as was mine.

The desert scenery was more of the same, but the highway was joyfully smooth. As we climbed up Kitt Peak, it became more cool and pleasant. Pulled into a picnic site with no signs saying, "Keep dogs on leash." Had lunch at a picnic table and let Ink explore. She stretched out on the cool ground under the table and enjoyed her freedom.

At the top of the mountain, it was very cool. Ink guarded the house and I went into the visitor center. Bought two Papago baskets. The price and selection were good. It was three o'clock and closing was at four. Asked a cute attendant which telescope he would visit if he could only see one. Felt that was all I had time for. He directed me to M-4, the biggest telescope in the array.

Walked to M-4 in heavy winds. When I got inside, I couldn't decipher the directional signs for the elevator and the viewing area. Was standing there feeling really dumb and not sure I could cope with this culture. A Mexican laborer walked by, looked at me, and asked if I was having *un problema*. I smiled and said, *"Estoy perdida."* He took me gently by the hand and led me to the elevator.

From the viewing area, I counted 13 different telescopes here on top of the mountain. It was impressive and very windy. I spent some time taking in this fine array of telescopes and "ears" peering out into the universe.

Back to Ink and Tessie and down the mountain. Pulled into a station for gas. No smiling lads came to greet me. I had to pump my own gas and paid $1.13 a gallon. Surely I was missing the Baja.

That night it was another circle. We stayed at Cactus Country on the east side of Tucson. Grounds were the same, lots of walking space for Ink, but the rate was now $14.50. Did a load of laundry, had a light meal, a stroll and bed.

# # #

Saturday morning, we left early. Stopped in Wilcox for supplies. Had a devil of a time with all the choices — so much stuff, so many decisions. Thought we'd check out Roper Lake north on Route 666. It looked like arid, dusty country and the wind was howling. Instead, turned west and into Coronado National Forest.

Stopped at Arcadia Campground and knew my guides were still with me. It was a primitive park filled with pine trees and plants in their fresh, spring foliage. It had been a long time since we had parked among the pines. The smell was heavenly. The grounds did not open officially until May first, so there were no fees, but there was water. Ink and I hiked and took deep breaths of that heavenly pine scent. Settled early with the wind whispering in the pines. Sounded better than the wind whispering in the palms.

Stayed Sunday at Arcadia and had a cool, pine-scented day. A few picnickers pulled into the park. By dusk, there was only the gypsy caravan. A crescent moon was shining through the pines. I built a fire. Sat and breathed deeply the welcome scents of wood smoke and pine needles. Turned in early and had a restful night. Was not anxious to get to Las Cruces and wondered why. Perhaps, I had been away too long.

# # #

Had a long conversation with myself at Arcadia the next morning. Decided I was hesitant to plunge back into the culture because I was afraid I would lose the beautiful balance and tranquility I had gained in Baja. Gave myself a pep talk: I would lose this peaceful feeling only if I let it happen. The decision was totally mine. That helped.

I decided we must move on. I had to get a new driver's license and had a multitude of friends waiting. Pulled out of that lovely campground and drove north though Safford and across high country.

We entered New Mexico at Mule Creek in the Gila area. The beauty and grandeur of the state still impressed me. The winds were beastly, but spring was coming. It was a fact of life that the winds howled over the land in the spring.

We stopped under a grove of cottonwoods and had lunch.

Then, into Silver City. Ink was suffering from dry skin and scratching uncontrollably. I picked up some Sulfodine and doused her liberally. It helped. Silver City was too busy for us. Drove down and stayed that night at City of Rocks State Park. I found a spot sheltered from the heavy winds by a boulder the size of an apartment building. Had a magnificent view of Cook's Peak. With sunset, the winds subsided and the night was serene. The moon and stars were brilliant. I was beginning to feel I was home.

# # #

May first, I drove into Deming. Called Sam and her joyous greeting warmed my heart. She asked when we'd arrive. I said we could make it that same evening. She was so elated that I finally looked forward to getting to Las Cruces.

Tess hummed the 60 miles on Interstate 25 and we arrived at Sam's about 6:30 p.m. My little family was fine and delighted to see me. Sam commented on my thinness with, "No one that thin can be healthy!" Told her I was fine and would try to fatten up and not dance as much.

That evening, after a good visit, I crawled into Tessie. Thanked gods, guides, and spirits for my interlude in Baja and Barrio San Ignacio. I knew I'd never forget it and was glad I had stayed in that paradise. Still, it was wonderful to be back with good friends and parked up with Sam and Theo. Once again, we were the guest house in the yard.

# # #

Postscript.

I tackled the Transpeninsular, for the second time, in December of 1993. This time in a 21-foot Toyota Oddyssey RV with two dogs — Ink and Negro — and about 150 pounds of donated clothes, shoes and toys for *mis vecinos* in the Barrio. It was a joyous reunion. I was delighted that

I was still welcomed with open arms.

But Todos Santos was changing. It has been discovered and was over-run with tourists during the season. Cerritos Beach, where I parked, was a mass of "pig-rigs" and not the tranquil setting I envisioned. Quite a few *extraños* had chosen to settle in my paradise. These changes were destined to come.

And now, Mexico has many problems; politically and economically. Although the peso has been devalued, prices have escalated. And, it is no longer the cheap vacation area it once was. *La gente* can barely afford food or gasoline. With these hardships, crime is on the rise — more on the mainland than Baja Sur. Politically, the changes are coming, too. In spite of most people in the US condemning the corruption in the Mexican government, I suggest they look closely at our own. Mexico does not interfere in the daily lives of its citizens as much as Big Brother.

One thing that hasn't changed: the bond is still strong between me and my barrio neighbors. Jorge and Elisa are well, Mirta has two more children, Mercedes and Carmila come home each year. Hermalinda, who writes me often, has a son, Jorge Raymundo, now six. I am honored to be his Aunt. We tease that I'm the *tía gringa*.

My dear friend El is still on the beach. We, too, stay in touch. She has not bought a house. Lives in her Airstream at Cerritos. Writes that the beach is overrun with "pig rigs" in season. I know I couldn't handle that, but it pleases me to know she's there — if and when I return.

Yes, I long for the Barrio and my pristine beach at times, but one can never recapture how it was. I left a part of my heart with the people there. I'm grateful for the time I had before it all changed.

Barb's First Book!

HOW CAN I BE LOST WHEN I DON'T KNOW WHERE I'M GOING?
Wandering Across the Continent with Barb Thacker and Her Dog, Ink

ISBN: 0-938513-20-6   290 pp. $14.00

From the southwest, north to Ontario, Quebec, and the Maritimes, back and forth across eastern and southern U.S., on a four-month trip, the author discovered that, in spite of what the media spew out, the world is still full of good, decent and caring people. The malaise of fear, suspicion and hostility gripping our nation prompted her to write this book to reaffirm the basic goodness of the human race. She suggests that we can set aside the paranoia and remember that we are all family.

Barbara Thacker is a traveler and a writer. She has two grown sons and a continuing interest in the human species. She now lives in Rio Rancho, New Mexico, when she's not on the road.

"This book shows rut-dwellers and rat-racers how to find freedom, independence and serenity in a way so simple it gets little attention."
— Robert Sowell, retired chemist and camper

"These 'Travels with Ink' are part of the new literature about the RV culture — a world that shows Americans mostly at their best."
— Joan M. Jensen, Professor Emerita, NMSU

INKWELL PRESS
P. O. Box 44817
Rio Ranchos, NM 87174-4817

ORDER BLANK

# of copies

____Blissfully Lost in the Baja
@ 15.00 _____

____How Can I Be Lost
@ 14.00 _____

Shipping & Handling   2.50

Total, enclosed   _____

Send to:

Name_____

Address_____

City, Zip, State_____